Carving Animal Canes & Walking Sticks with Power

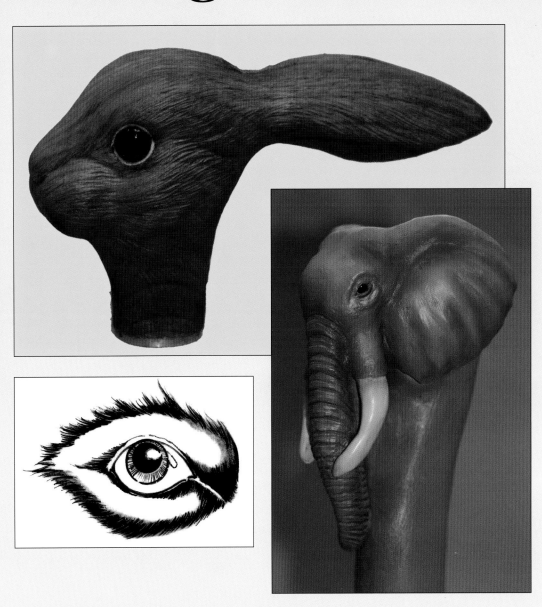

Frank C. Russell

4880 Lower Valley Road, Atglen, PA 19310 USA

Dedication

To *The Stonegate Woodcarving School (1995 – 2005)*
- for the cherished friends it has made,
- for the amazing students it has produced,
- for the remarkable opportunities it has granted,
- for the quality of life it has afforded.

Published by Schiffer Publishing Ltd.
4880 Lower Valley Road
Atglen, PA 19310
Phone: (610) 593-1777; Fax: (610) 593-2002
E-mail: Info@schifferbooks.com

For the largest selection of fine reference books on this and related subjects, please visit our web site at
www.schifferbooks.com
We are always looking for people to write books on new and related subjects. If you have an idea for a book please contact us at the above address.

This book may be purchased from the publisher.
Include $3.95 for shipping.
Please try your bookstore first.
You may write for a free catalog.

In Europe, Schiffer books are distributed by
Bushwood Books
6 Marksbury Ave.
Kew Gardens
Surrey TW9 4JF England
Phone: 44 (0) 20 8392-8585; Fax: 44 (0) 20 8392-9876
E-mail: info@bushwoodbooks.co.uk
Free postage in the U.K., Europe; air mail at cost.

Designed by Mark David Bowyer
Type set in Americana XBd BT/Humanist 521 BT

ISBN: 0-7643-2381-4
Printed in China

Contents

Foreword

I hope you enjoy the cane and walking stick patterns I have presented in this book. Primary attention has been given to carving the decorative aspects of canes and sticks – most especially the carving of cane heads and handles.

I have tried to demonstrate a diversity of animals that will allow each carver to begin with a type of creature to his or her liking. The patterns, along with the carving and painting sequences that accompany them, are meant to instruct in the basics of cane or stick head carving. Hopefully, what is contained herein will not only provide the groundwork to allow anyone to carve a beautiful and functional cane or walk-ing stick from the patterns provided in this book, but will encourage them to originate and create heirloom canes and walking sticks of their own.

Again, please be advised that the primary purpose of this book is the carving and adornment of cane handles and walk-ing stick heads, and to that end is directed only in part at the *construction* of canes and walking sticks. Suggestions, hardware, and/or some accessories have been given or illustrated to provoke thought with respect to completion. Once a handle or head is carved, the reader is left to his own devices as to the completion of the project

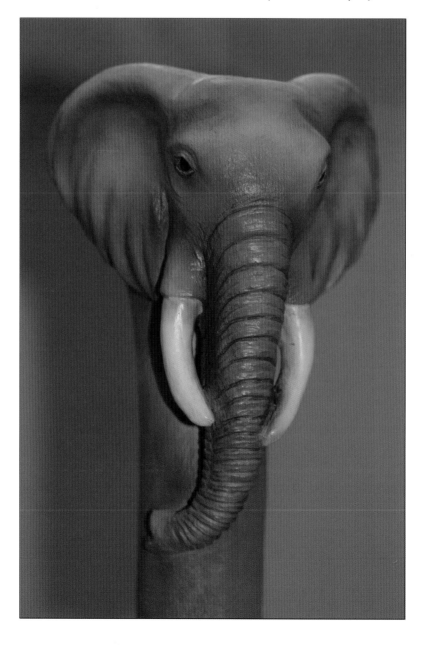

Types of Cane Handles

The type of cane handle you choose to carve for yourself or for a client should be chosen to first provide comfort while in use, second, to have the strength overall to withstand use, and finally, to have an attractive appearance. No matter how nice a cane looks, it gives little to the user if it is uncomfortable to handle. Conversely, if a cane is comfortable to use, and looks nice, but is too spindly or ill-designed for the user to put necessary weight on or against, it becomes useless as well as dangerous.

The type and shape of handle you choose to carve may also have a lot to do with how the cane will be used or carried. If a person needs a cane with a handle that will provide sufficient grip to him/her to walk, the choice may be vastly different than a cane that rarely touches the ground, such as one carried to accent formal attire or one that is carried "just in case" to keep an errant dog at bay while taking an afternoon walk around the neighborhood.

The seven cane handle patterns that follow, and a few suggested carving applications, may be of assistance when designing or choosing a cane to carve for a specific client or a specific use.

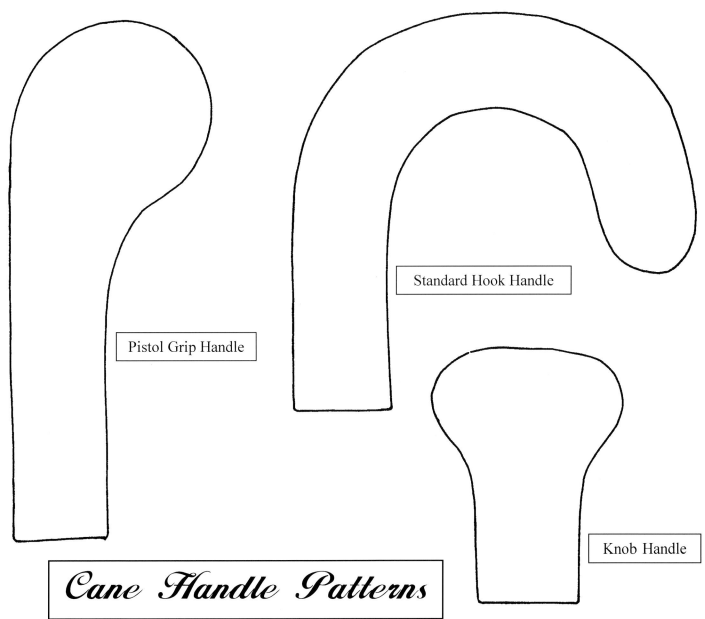

Standard Hook Handle

Pistol Grip Handle

Knob Handle

Cane Handle Patterns

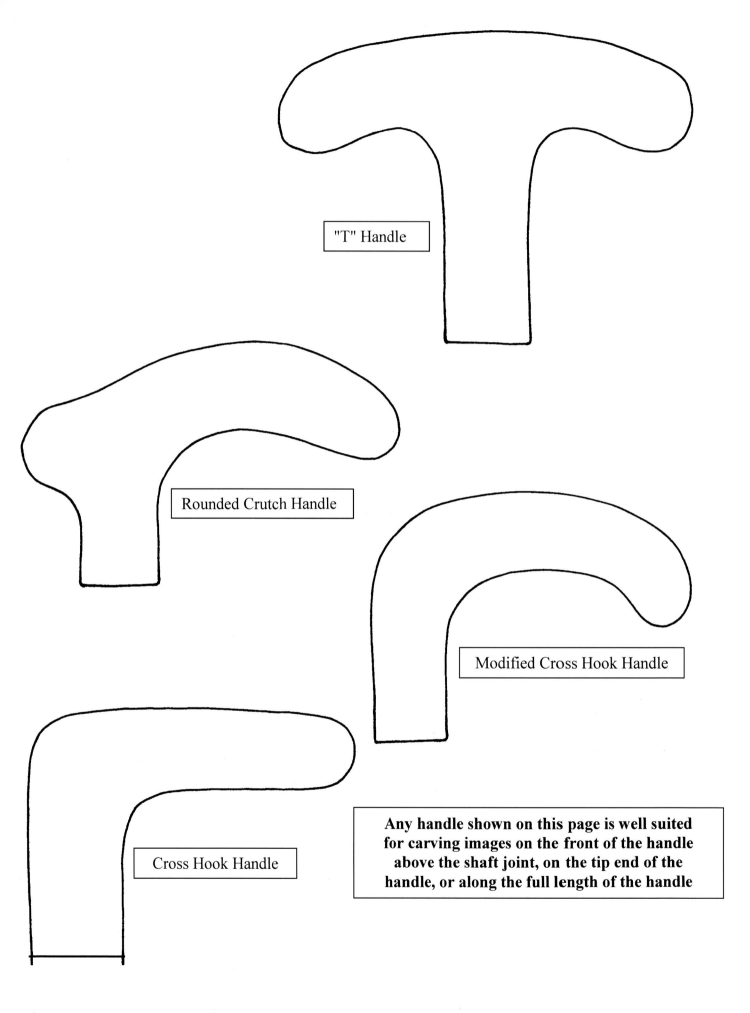

"T" Handle

Rounded Crutch Handle

Modified Cross Hook Handle

Cross Hook Handle

Any handle shown on this page is well suited for carving images on the front of the handle above the shaft joint, on the tip end of the handle, or along the full length of the handle

Subject Placement

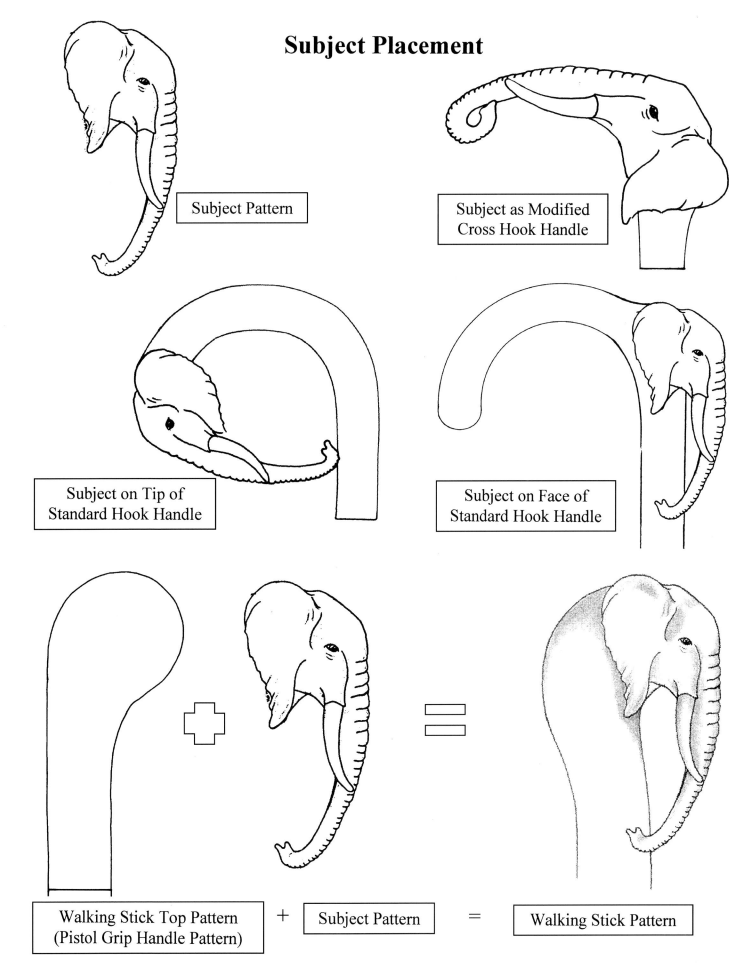

Subject Pattern

Subject as Modified
Cross Hook Handle

Subject on Tip of
Standard Hook Handle

Subject on Face of
Standard Hook Handle

Walking Stick Top Pattern
(Pistol Grip Handle Pattern)   +   Subject Pattern   =   Walking Stick Pattern

Figure 3

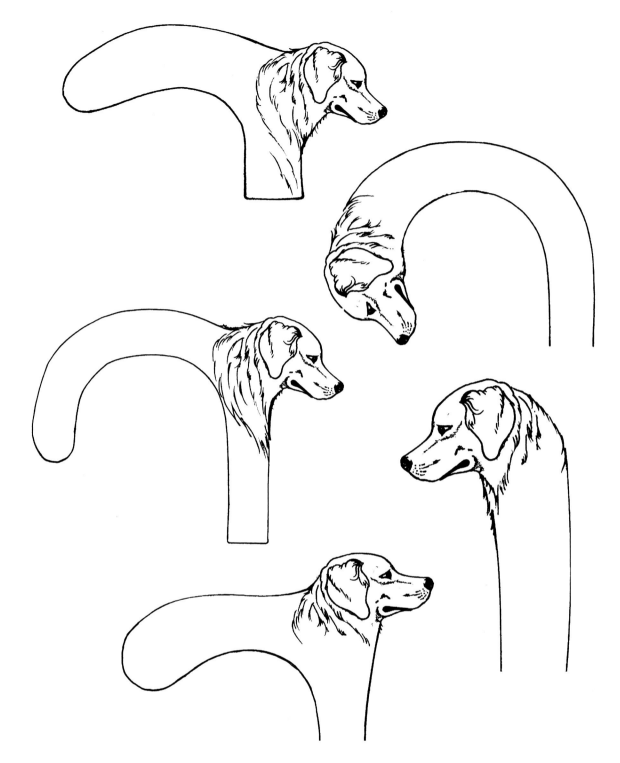

Figure 4

Cane Shafts

Dowel Shafts

The simplest way to achieve a cane shaft is to attach your carved cane head to a 3/4-inch dowel rod using brass cane hardware with a 3/4-inch collar. I made a jig for my drill press that allows me to slide the dowel up through a hole in the jig, clamp the dowel in place, and drill a hole into the end of the dowel not only centered, but to proper depth (using the depth stop on the drill press) and size using the proper sized bit to drill a hole that the hardware fits into.

I first started using 3/4-inch diameter x 36-inch long birch dowels purchased from local hardware stores and lumber companies, then staining the birch to match as closely as I could the cane head I had carved. It wasn't long before I found all kinds of dowel companies on the internet and now I have ready sources of supply for walnut, cherry, oak, maple, and other domestic and exotic woods that are offered.

For a minimum price (at this point in time I am paying two to five dollars – depending on the wood the dowel is made from) I get a ready-made cane shaft that only requires light sanding, a finish application, and waxing, and I am ready to assemble my cane components and size the cane to the client. The finished shaft is attractive as well as offering function and quality in a minimum of time – thanks to the dowels.

I often carve designs and figures on and along these dowel shafts to exemplify the theme or subject of the cane head.

Natural Shafts

The easiest shaft to create is a length of sapling of preferred diameter cut to the desired length. Choose one that is as straight as possible, because the more bends, the more vibrations that are delivered to the wrist through that cane or walking stick. With the bark left on, this particular shaft lends itself very well to bird, animal, and nature carving themes. The first Cardinal walking stick that I carved from the pattern shown in a preceding book, *Carving Wildfowl Canes and Walking Sticks* (Schiffer Publishing) was carved from a natural sapling, and I left bark on the entire length of the shaft, leaving only natural wood for the carved cardinal stick head, and the handle/thong area.

To insure that the bark will adhere to the shaft over time, I seal the entire shaft with thinned flat lacquer to seal and lock it into place. I use several coats of automotive lacquer thinned 50% with lacquer thinner.

Most of the shafts I use have had the bark removed from them – especially if I plan to carve along the length of the shaft. I use a spoke shave or a draw knife to strip the bark away, then I allow the shaft to dry for a while if the shaft has been cut in the spring or summer while sap is flowing in the sapling. A drier shaft is easier to work with respect to shaping than is a freshly cut wet shaft. I have found the best time to cut saplings for walking sticks is during the late fall or winter when the sap has stopped flowing.

I once carved a wizard head cane (pattern to be found in a forthcoming book). I used the bent root section of the sapling as the handle, which was also his hat, carved his head and face at the bend, and then had a beard that spiraled all the way from his face to the tip of the cane. Never again will I carve a wizard cane or walking stick like that! Shaping and rough carving the spiraled beard was enjoyable, but detailing all the hair on that long, long spiraling beard became agony. The man that owns that cane has often asked me to carve a matching walking stick for him...which would mean a beard almost five feet long! I get cramps just thinking about it!

Sawn Shaft

An attractive shaft can be made by first rip sawing (cutting along the length with the grain) a length of stock to an octagonal shape. This is accomplished by first sawing the stock square, then setting the saw blade at a 45° angle and ripping all four corners to form the eight equal sides of an octagon. The eight flats of the shaft can then be smoothed by running opposing sides through a planer with the planer head set to the desired thickness, or the entire shaft can be hand sanded using a sanding block and honoring the flat surfaces.

This type of staff will require the cane or stick head and/or handle being added – but for a walking stick, it allows the shaft to be shaped to full length without joinery anywhere along its length. I think shaping a shaft using this method gives the cane a more formal look. I especially like to "dress" a cane shaft with an opposing colored tip and collar before I add a handle – for example, a walnut shaft with maple collar and tip.

Turned Shaft

Many shafts for canes and walking sticks are turned on a lathe. This method affords the stick or cane maker the greatest variety and choice of shaft. The shaft of a cane can be turned tapered or straight, it can be ornamented with grooves or raised rings, and finally, it can be finish coated – all while in place on the lathe.

I have not yet been able to find (or afford) a non-commercial lathe with a bed long enough to turn the full length of a walking stick shaft (60"-65").

I have tried to purchase 60-inch tapered shafts for walking sticks from companies that turn the larger decorative posts for porches and railings, but understandably, the price was prohibitive for the few pieces that I wanted.

To date, I have used two methods to create walking stick shafts on a short-bed lathe (36" length). One method is to turn half-lengths of the shaft and join them with a doweled glue joint (usually with a fancy wood spacer between them). The second method is to make a "take-down" screw joint, which allows the user to assemble and disassemble the walking stick in the same manner that one would assemble a pool cue. During the nineteenth century, canes with a joint like this were known as "traveling sticks."

Many of the hikers and outdoors folks prefer the takedown type because it can be disassembled and easily transported. Whereas most of those that just take a daily walk around the neighborhood prefer the fixed length of a walking stick because it is usually left leaning in the same place each day (a corner, behind a door, a coat closet) where it provides easy access.

Most of the cane heads and walking stick heads that I carve, are screw-on heads with a female threaded insert. I like the idea of being able to use the same shaft with different heads that I have carved. When I go for a walk or a hike, I enjoy having a different subject with me each time. Most importantly, when I walk or hike, I usually have my camera with me, and the threaded metal pin that sticks out of the top of the walking stick shaft and screws into the stick head, also fits my camera. All I have to do is unscrew the carved head, screw on my camera, and I have a nice monopod with which to steady my camera.

When turning a walking stick that I intend to use as a camera monopod, I turn a handle area that will have finger grooves. These grooves not only allow a tangible grip while the camera is mounted, but provide a comfortable handle to grasp while hiking. A common mistake for beginning stickmakers is to leave the shaft too thick and too heavy to be a comfort while in use. The finished stick must be an object of function as well as one of beauty.

Routed Shaft

A routed shaft is one that is routed with a router and bit on all four corners.

Before attempting to route a shaft for a cane or walking stick, I provide additional support for the router. This support is usually nothing more than another piece of stock of equal thickness to the shaft blank that is clamped or screwed to the bench alongside the shaft blank. Once the blank is clamped in place, the blank and the adjacent piece of stock both act as supporting surfaces for the router to ride on. The "fixture" supports the shaft blank while I shape each corner with whatever router bit shape I have selected.

Some bit shapes that lend themselves very well to shaping this type of shaft are quarter round, quarter concave, 45-degree bevel, or even some of the more ornate router bit shapes that will satisfy the corner shaping that you might prefer on the shaft. Always use bits with roller bearings on them, or use an edge guide on your router.

A floor-mounted shaper may also be used to shape the edges of this type of cane shaft, but I find the router more versatile if I am making a tapered cane shaft. The shaper will give as fine a finish, but the main problem is setting the hold down guides properly and feeding the shaft by the cutter head. Even with push sticks I don't like my hands/fingers that close to that cutter head!

Tool Handle Shaft

I must admit that I have made some rather remarkable walking sticks and canes with carved heads from unfinished broom, mop, and rake handles that I have found at the local hardware store. I have also made several nice walking sticks and canes from old pool cues. Pool cue walking sticks can be easily unscrewed and stored in an auto for transportation. Even better if one has the partitioned box that the cue came in.

It is a simple chore to drill a hole the same size as the broomstick in the bottom of the carved stick head, and glue the head to the stick. After finish is applied to the stick, I wrap the grip area with rawhide thong or a wide leather flat lace to provide a handgrip (with or without a wrist loop). After adding a rubber crutch or cane tip, the project is complete.

Don't be afraid to "collar" the tip down as necessary to make the rubber crutch or cane tip fit. The fit should be as snug as possible, but not left so big as to eventually split the rubber tip from use and/or the user leaning on it.

Joinery Tools, Hardware, & Accessories

The author wishes to thank Lee Valley Tools Ltd. for providing all the cane hardware featured.

Couplers

Couplers are excellent for joining the handle of a cane to a cane shaft, or the carved head of a walking stick to a shaft.

With a coupler, additional length can be added to a cane shaft to convert it to a walking stick in the same manner that a pool cue is screwed together. A walking stick with a coupler can be easily broken down for easy transport or stowage in a carrying case.

The coupler shown is an assembly consisting of two 1-inch long by 7/16-inch diameter nuts connected by a 3-20 threaded joining screw.

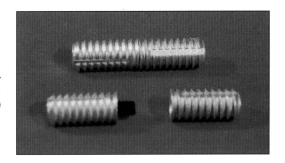

A walking stick can easily be converted to a camera mount monopod by unscrewing the carved stick head and mounting a camera on the exposed threaded screw sticking up from the center of the shaft of the walking stick. These camera mount couplers have two 7/16-inch diameter nuts (one 2-inch long and the other 1-inch long), and are joined by a 3-20 threaded stud.

Note: Both video cameras and 35mm cameras have 1/4-20 threaded mounting holes.

This camera mount is invaluable when I am doing photography for carving references at zoos, sanctuaries, game refuges, or in any situation where I need a stable support for shooting photographs.

Joining Plates

Joining plates are available with 1-inch and 3/4-inch plates. These are excellent for those who wish to make segmented canes or walking sticks, or desire hardware for mounting handles to canes or heads to walking sticks. When joined, the brass plate makes a very attractive spacer between the two pieces being joined.

Cane Tips

Cane tips are added to the tips (bottom) of cane shafts to prevent wear and erosion of the cane shaft as it is placed repeatedly against the ground. In addition to protection, the tip also should provide a degree of traction to prevent the cane from sliding out from under the weight applied by the user.

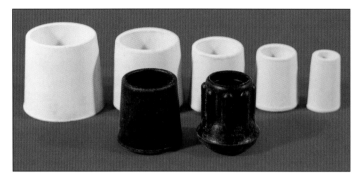

The most common tips are the rubber crutch-type tips that are easily slid on the cane shaft and held in place by friction and/or a drop of Super Glue™. These rubber tips are available in a variety of sizes and colors (predominately black, brown, or white). The ones shown were purchased at a flea market, priced from thirty-cents to sixty-cents apiece. The larger ones are well suited for use on the ends of larger walking sticks.

To add more quality to a cane, brass or other metals are an excellent choice. The usual choice is brass, but I have had stainless steel tips turned for canes where I wanted a silver color to enhance the look of the wood. On several occasions I even made silver tips from jewelry stock for cane tips where the cane was never used, but added to a collection. As previously stated, the more commonly used metal for a tip is brass.

A so-called traditional British cane tip is available which is made from drawn brass with a steel disc welded to the bottom to prevent wear. These tips are approximately 1-inch high, are slightly tapered, and are usually available in 9/16-inch, 5/8-inch, and 3/4-inch sizes. The tip is set with epoxy or a brass pin or brad. These tips add greatly to the beauty and presentation of a cane, but for those who would depend on a cane for function and support, I have concerns about the lack of traction due to the smoothness of the steel-plated tip.

An excellent and versatile tip for a staff or walking stick is a brass tip that has not only a rubber tip for path or sidewalk walking, but has an interchangeable stainless steel tip that can be added for stream walking or mountain trekking. These tips are 1 1/4-inches long, and fit a shaft end with a diameter of 3/4-inch or larger. They are scored internally to provide a mechanical lock for gluing and have internally chamfered lips for a snug fit. For extreme use, the addition of a pin should be considered – if you subject the tip of a walking stick to the horrors of water, mud, gravel, ice, and snow that I do.

Tenon Cutters

These cutters are designed to run vibration free while being driven by an electric drill. They cut a nice smooth tenon with a slight radius on the shoulder. These cutters offer a broad range of sizes to satisfy about any size shaft that would be used for a cane or walking stick. There are mini sizes (1/4", 3/8", 1/2", 9/16") and larger sizes (5/8", 3/4", 7/8", 1", 1 1/2", 2") – with 5/8" through 1" most suitable for cane and stick making. They are not for use in a drill press – the smaller sizes (up to 1-inch) are used in an electric drill with a 3/8-inch or larger chuck, and the larger sizes are for use in an electric hand drill with a 1/2-inch chuck.

The best brass cane tips are machine-turned from bar stock to insure quality and uniformity, and are fitted with replaceable rubber tips that provide the desired traction. This is my choice for the majority of canes that I create that have metal tips. They are 3/4-inch in length and fit cane shaft ends with a diameter of 5/8-inch or larger. The tip has a heavy-duty replaceable rubber tip with a fixing screw.

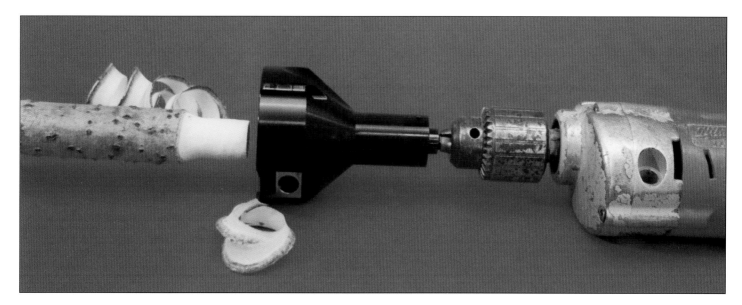

I have used them for everything from furniture making and repair to cane and walking stick construction. These bits will easily shape a male end on a piece of wood stock that will fit a corresponding hole to make an extremely strong and tidy joint for canes, walking sticks, or furniture.

Once the male end is made, a hole of corresponding size is drilled using a Forstner drill bit (see below), and the two are glue joined to make a very secure and attractive joint. I have used them time and time again to join cane and stick heads.

Forstner Bits

These bits drill flat-bottomed holes that accept dowels or tenoned ends of shafts to form a strong joint when glued.

Forstner bits are available in a wide range of sizes. Economically, sets of bits are far cheaper than buying individual bits.

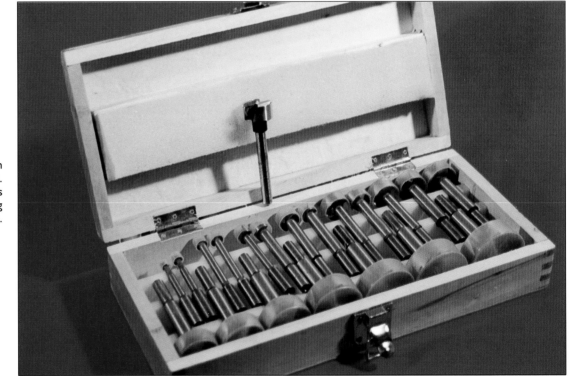

The Tenon Cutters and Forstner Bits featured above and all cane tips and joiners are available from:
Lee Valley Tools Ltd.
814 Proctor Avenue
Ogdensburg, New York 13669-2205
www.leevalley.com

All preparation for joinery (joining a handle or head to a shaft) should be fitted and complete before cutting or carving the head/handle and shaft components of a cane or walking stick. It is much easier to drill and fit rough squared stock than it is to try to work around a beautifully carved handle and shaped shaft. This applies to any case whether it be a piece of square stock to be turned on the lathe, squared stock to be corner-shaped with a router or shaper, or even a natural sapling to be used for a walking stick. *Always* fit the roughed out components to be joined before carving and finish shaping.

Carving Tools & Machines

Flexible Shaft Machine

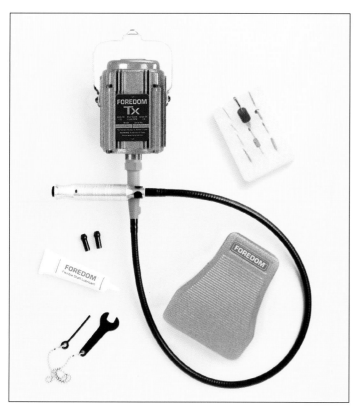

The Flexible shaft machine used to rough out and initial shaping of all the projects in this book is the Foredom TX Machine.

The TX models are Foredom's most powerful flex shaft machines and, at this writing, are relatively new to the market. I prefer the TX for the torque and speed it gives me as compared to most other flex machines. They have permanent magnet DC ball-bearing motors with rare earth magnets in place of wound fields. It must be noted that they do not feature a reverse mode, but do deliver more torque not only at low speed, but throughout the entire speed range, than do standard universal motors of the same size. They also feature standard flexible shafts and sheaths for connecting to any "quick disconnect" hand pieces. The TX unit uses either a foot or tabletop speed control that is specific to this machine and provides TX-specific electronics for smoother acceleration and better control of the tool under any load.

A note about left-handed use...

Reverse is not that important for the right-handed carver, but is of utmost importance to the left-handed carver. To allow the left-handed carver the same rotational privilege as the right-hander, the machine should be run in reverse. By necessity, the bit should be turning towards the carver whether left- or right-handed, and in order for the left-hander to get the machine to run towards him, the machine must be running in reverse. This allows monitoring of the bottom of the bit where the cut is taking place, and the left-hander is not fighting the direction of the bit that would try to run away from him if it were not in reverse.

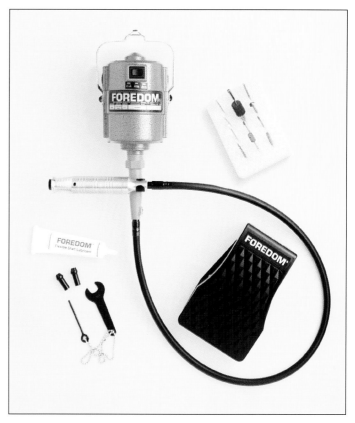

Another machine for right-handers, *but* very well suited to those left-handers who must run their machines in reverse and that I would highly recommend, is Foredom's SR machine.

Due to the mix of left- and right-handed students I expected and have had at my school for the past twelve years, I equipped each carving position with an SR machine – *the "S" stands for the model, and the "R" means it has a reverse.* These machines have proven to be absolute workhorses over the years and have withstood the misuse and abuse dished out in ways that only unknowing beginning students can produce. With 1/8 horsepower, these machines easily supply more than enough power necessary to rough out any band-sawn carving blank (to the size of a full-scale swan!) with ease and accuracy when provided with the proper bit.

Two handpieces (large and small) make the reducing and shaping of stock much easier – the large handpiece easily takes care of wasting away and rough shaping, and the smaller handpiece is a more convenient size for continued wasting away and the refining of rough shaped details.

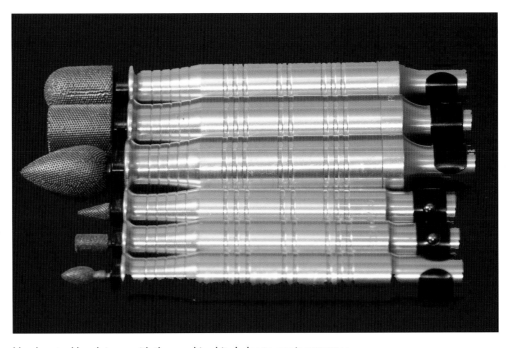

I load several handpieces with the roughing bits I plan to use in sequence so I won't have to take the time to stop and reload a new bit every time I have a bit change. For years, I made a point of picking up an extra handpiece…then another…then another…etc. (*my wife says I employ the same approach to boats, fishing gear, and hunting gear*).

For a more complete explanation for these machines as well as all Foredom machines, bits, and accessories, log on to their website at www.foredom.com or, for a catalog, contact:
Foredom Electric Company
16 Stony Hill Road
Bethel, Connecticut 06801-1039

Micromotor Machine

The motor in this machine is definitely not for roughing out large shapes as are the flexible shaft machines featured above; however, the high speed of this machine and the range of freedom of the handpiece allow for fine detailing and, generally, a smoother cut. This was the machine of choice for all the light carving, detailing, and texturing used on the projects throughout this book.

The Gesswein Power Hand® 2X Standard Controller & Handpiece(s)

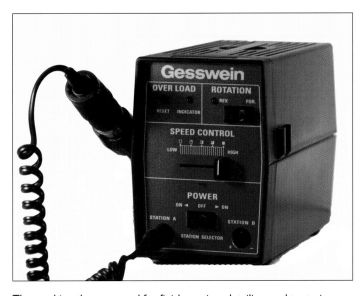

The machine that was used for finish carving, detailing, and texturing some of the projects in this book is the Gesswein Power Hand® 2X – a micromotor that I have set up with two handpieces, one that revolves at 55,000 rpm (revolutions per minute) and the other that revolves at 35,000 rpm – plus a third handpiece with a slim-line head for deep and/or narrow reach.

A complete Power Hand® station, consists of a controller (control box) and one or two handpieces connected to the control box with power cords. As the name implies, the controller provides controls such as on/off, variable speed, and forward/reverse to the handpiece, which houses the rotary drive motor and bit collet (bit holder).

Several handpiece options are available for specific bit applications as well as optional on/off foot control and/or foot speed control.

Both standard and dual controllers feature:

High torque at constant RPM.

Quick-change tool mechanism.

Vibration-free, true-running operation.

Variable speeds.

Telephone-type cord for easy reaching – extends to 6 feet.

Air-cooled 30VDC (Volts Direct Current) motor in handpieces.

Lightweight and comfortable to grip.

Overload protection.

The standard Controller is designed for one-person use, but has two output stations with a switch to instantly change power from one handpiece to the other. Speed can be adjusted by a slide rheostat or an optional foot rheostat. The panel also has an on/off switch, a convenient forward/reverse switch, and the unit housing features a wonderfully convenient and adjustable handpiece holder on either side.

Specifications

Electrical:	115V or 230V AC, 50/60Hz
Output Voltage:	3 – 30V DC
Dimensions:	3-3/8"W x 7-3/4"D x 5-3/4"H
Net Weight:	5-1/2 lbs.

Both Standard and Dual Controllers will accept any of the Power Hand 2X Handpieces and offer the option of a foot rheostat and/or on-off foot switch.

Power Hand 2X Handpieces have a built-in electric motor and connect to the compact portable controller with a telephone-type coil cord.

These handpieces fit your fingers like a pen and are exceptionally true-running and vibration-free. They are sturdy and durable yet lightweight and well-balanced. They feature a unique quick-change bit mechanism that minimizes interruption while carving. And importantly, they are quiet and run cool during use.

Over the past fourteen years that I have had occasion to use these machines, I have had to change the bearings in a handpiece but one time, and the controller still remains virtually maintenance free. All this being said, I hasten to add that I maintain a continuous habit of cleaning and the application of care recommended by the manufacturer. It must be kept in mind that these machines are made for light-duty carving such as finish detail carving and texturing, as opposed to wasting away large quantities of stock from a band sawn carving blank.

A more complete explanation for this machine as well as all other Gesswein products (bits, machines, & accessories) may be obtained from their website at www.Gesswein.com or writing for a catalog to:

Paul H. Gesswein & Co. Inc.
255 Hancock Avenue
Bridgeport, CT 06605

Wood Burning

Burning Pens

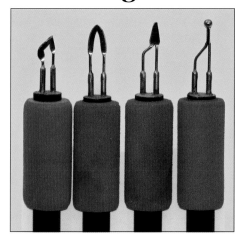

The burning pen shapes I use regularly to cover any aspect of woodburning required for animal, fish, or reptile carving are the large skew, spear point, small rounded skew, and various sizes of ball points. I use burning pens to a far greater extent on bird carvings than I do on animal carvings because I prefer to texture hair and fur with a texturing bit. Albeit I often use burning pens on mammals to exemplify areas of fur that I feel need a deeper, narrower, or more pronounced detail than I can achieve with a standard texturing stone.

The large skew enjoys the greatest amount of use for the type of woodburning I do because it is the most versatile and lends itself well to accentuating hair and fur details, deepening cuts, undercutting, and "cauterizing" claws and teeth. *When I cauterize, I use a low heat setting, and rub the side of the pen over the claw or tooth to give it a hard, smooth surface.*

Spear point tip – This shape is also good for undercutting curls, smoothing out, outlining/shaping, and accentuating.

Small rounded skew tip – I reshaped this point very slightly on the tip because it felt more comfortable to me. Where necessary, it allows me to make the smallest of curved or straight lines and undercuts. Excellent for use when I need to exemplify fine-hair areas of stone texturing on heads, capes, tails, and in and around ears.

Ball tip – this tip is available in different ball sizes and can be used to draw lines, shade, and do reproductive shading/texturing. I go to the ball bits to outline and establish a scale pattern from the smallest scales to the largest of fish scales. I have ground and filed the 1/8" size into various shapes that I needed to accomplish various indentation shapes and repetitive patterns. I hollowed a large ball on one side and have used that bit to create everything from beads on an Indian carving to the dimpled texture of a football used in a carving.

The pens shown are manufactured by the company shown below, and product information and pricing can be obtained at:

PJL Enterprises
PO Box 273, 720 North Perry Ave.
Browerville, MN 56438
or through their website:
www.carvertools.com

Control Box

A control box must generate an even and constant source of power to the pen and have a quick recovery time as the pen is repeatedly cooled during the texturing process. At a minimum, features I look for on the face of the box are an ON/OFF switch *separate* from a heat adjustment indicator and a pilot light that tells me whether the unit is on or off.

The heat setting indicator should be separate from the ON/OFF switch simply because once I begin burn texturing, I usually have occasion to turn the unit off and on several times during the course of texturing the project. I want the setting to be the same each time I turn the unit back on, and unless I can leave it set in the same place, most of the time I can't remember what setting it was on when I turned it off. Some boxes have the ON/OFF switch and heat setting indication combined on one knob.

I like a pilot light on the control face of the unit because there are times when I forget to turn the unit off, and a brightly lit pilot light gives warning that the unit is *not* off. The last thing I do at anytime that I finish work in the studio is to scan my work area for any lit pilot lights.

I like the control box shown, also manufactured by *PJL Enterprises*, due to the fact that it is small, light, and very portable, yet has enough power to satisfy the demands of my heaviest pens. It performs well enough that every carving station at my woodcarving school has one.

Bits & Bit Use

I include the following section regarding bit uses, bit shapes, and bit descriptions primarily to cover the bits that were used for the projects in this book to help clarify bit choice – and to answer some of the hundreds of questions I am asked about bits during seminars, demonstrations, and classes.

Bit Selection

The wrong selection of bits for a particular application is usually the reason many beginning woodcarvers get a poor result on a project, give up on a project, or even give up on power carving. If the bit fails to function as it should, and/or fails to give the desired result, the carver is wasting time as well as effort and materials. Having stated all of this, let me hasten to say that in some cases, what will function perfectly for one carver won't do as well for another, due to carving technique and/or machinery. It remains for the individual to *experiment and practice* to learn how bits function and how bits are used to achieve desired results, and/or specific results.

Bit Shapes

The following bit shapes and uses are included to assist in the selection of bits according to the function that needs to be accomplished. When considering the cut to be made, give consideration to the size of the bit, the aggressiveness of the bit, the cutting surface and/or grit, and the desired result. The first six groups of bits feature the most commonly used shapes of bits in various sizes, materials, and grits. They are in no particular order of use with exception of the flame shaped bits which I consider the most important of all the shapes and use about ninety-percent of the time. The remaining single item bit photos are readily available but not in as wide a range of materials or sizes as are the first shapes.

If I didn't have flame shaped bits with which to carve, I probably wouldn't carve with power to the extent that I do. The flame is the most versatile shape of all, in that it has the ability to make three of the most used cuts accurately.

When used with a drag stroke* while cutting a V-groove with the tip or a U-groove with the barrel, the flame has the ability to relieve itself away from the cut without jumping out of line. I say this as long as the user doesn't exceed a cut much over the radius of the widest part of the flame. With any other shape, once a cut approaches a depth equal to the radius, enough friction is introduced on both sides of the bit to cause it to "chatter" and jump out of the cut line. *A drag stroke is made in the same manner that one would draw the base line of the letter "T" without crossing the T.*

The three functions of a flame shaped bit are illustrated as follows: First, while using a drag stroke with the handpiece held at a high angle and using the tip of the bit, the flame can execute a "V" groove such as one would cut with a V-gouge or parting tool by hand.

Flame Shapes –

- V-bottom cuts (handpiece held at high angle, using drag stroke)
- U bottom cuts (handpiece held at low angle, using drag stroke)
- general shaping
- detail shaping
- wasting away stock
- wasting away stock in recessed areas
- shaping and relieving away raised areas (i.e. eye mounds, muscle bulges, feather groups)

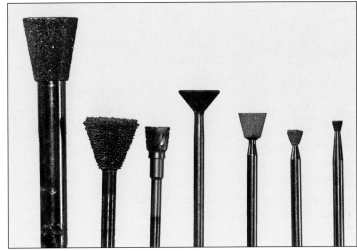

Inverted Cone –

— V-bottom cuts
— texturing feathers, fur, & hair
— undercutting raised areas
— relieving away
— v-cut outlining
Most common in the middle to smaller sizes of diamonds & stones – readily obtainable in 3/32" & 1/8" shafts

Secondly, while using a drag stroke with the handpiece held at a low angle and using the barrel or side of the bit, the flame can execute a "U" groove such as one would cut with a U-gouge by hand.

Finally, while using a wiping or side-to-side stroke with the section between the tip and the extreme of the barrel, the flame can be used to waste away in the same manner that one would use a knife to get rid of stock.

Ball Shape –

— relieving eye holes for setting glass eyes
— u-cut outlining & relieving away
— shaping and deepening hole shapes in nostrils, ears
— shaping and deepening shapes such as clothing wrinkles
— shaping and raising feather edges
— wasting away stock in recessed areas
— shaping and relieving away raised areas such as eye mounds, muscle bulges
— writing or scrolling words, symbols, monograms, designs, or insignia
Very common shape for all materials, sizes, and grits – readily obtainable with 3/32", 1/8", & 1/4" shafts

Obviously a combination of other bits can accomplish the same strokes, but only the flame can accomplish all three cuts with ease and without changing to a different bit shape. This shape alone can cut the same as three hand tools: the V-gouge, the U-gouge, and the knife.

Cylinder Shape –

— V-bottom cuts (v-cut outlining – handpiece held at high angle, using side stroke(s))
— wasting away flattened areas
— surface shaping
— texturing feathers, fur, & hair
Very common shape for all materials, sizes, and grits – readily obtainable with 3/32", 1/8", & 1/4" shafts

Taper Shape –

— general shaping
— detail shaping feather edges and surfaces
— u-cut outlining & relieving away
— wasting away stock
— shaping individual feathers and feather groups
Very common shape for all materials, sizes, and grits – readily obtainable with 3/32", 1/8", & 1/4" shafts

Bud Shape –

— shallow V-bottom cuts (held at high angle, using drag stroke)
— U bottom cuts (held at low angle, using drag stroke)
— general shaping
— detail shaping
— wasting away stock
— wasting away stock in recessed areas
— shaping and relieving away raised areas (i.e. eye mounds, muscle bulges)
More common in the middle to smaller sizes of steel burrs, ruby bits, and diamonds bits – readily obtainable in 3/32" & 1/8" shafts.

Ball Nose Shape –

— shaping with flat side or nose end of bit
— relieving raised/rounded contours
— establishing U-grooves/channels
— pre-texturing rough or to suggest textured fur & hair
Very common shape for all materials, sizes, and grits – readily obtainable with 3/32", 1/8", & 1/4" shafts

Inverted Pear Shape –

— establishing and enlarging "U" cuts or grooves
— relieving and raising contours
Generally in the middle to smaller sizes of steel burrs, ruby bits, diamonds bits, & stones – common with 3/32" & 1/8" shafts

Pear Shape –

— relieving and raising areas
— rounding relieved areas
— shaping with straight portion of profile
More common in the middle to smaller sizes of steel burrs, ruby bits, and diamond bits – readily obtainable in 3/32" & 1/8" shafts.

Oval Shape –

— general relieving
— detailing
— relieving raised/rounded contours
— establishing U-grooves/channels
Generally in the middle to smaller sizes of steel burrs, ruby bits, & diamonds bits – common with 3/32" & 1/8" shafts

Spear Point Shape –

— undercutting
— sharp indentations
— sharp deep V cuts
Generally in the middle to smaller sizes of steel burrs, diamond bit, & stones – common with 3/32" & 1/8" shafts

Bits Used for Projects

Roughing Bits

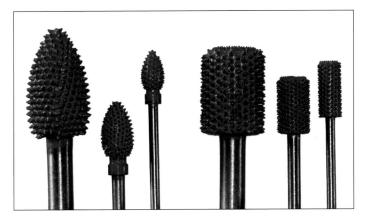

Coarse Carbide Burrs

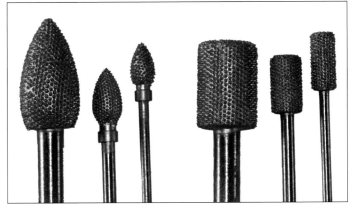

Fine Carbide Burrs

These bits are made for wasting away and for rough to moderately fine shaping, depending on the size of the burr and the detail of the carving. They are available in 1/4", 1/8", and 3/32" shafts in a fairly large variety of sizes and shapes. The coarse grit is an aggressive bit that may be a little too aggressive for some beginning carvers. I usually have my students try both before they invest – those with a more delicate touch (female carvers seem to have a lighter touch) or those who fear removing too much stock to begin with, often prefer the finer burrs.

Depending on the size of the flame shape being used, these bits are all excellent for initiating cuts/shapes, making V-Cuts and U-cuts, and shaping contours.

The cylinder shapes, again, depending on size, are used for wasting away on flats with the side and V-cuts with the top corner.

Detailing Bits

Ruby Carvers

Usually, ruby carvers have 3/32" diameter shafts and come in a large variety of shapes and sizes in fine, medium, and coarse grits. The bit itself consists of the metal shaft and a metal head that has been encrusted with graded commercial ruby chips.

The two shapes in various sizes and grits of ruby carvers used throughout this book are pretty much the same that I use for the majority of carving that I do. The large flame ruby (1/4" x 3/8") was used for general wasting away and refining shapes, and the small flame ruby (1/8" x 5/16") was used for defining and detailing shapes. The large ball shape (1/4" diameter) is used where larger eye cavities are required and to accentuate rounded and indented areas. The small ball shape (1/8" diameter) was used for outlining shapes, pre-contouring hair shapes and direction, and cutting eyeholes. See "Setting Glass Eyes" on page 31.

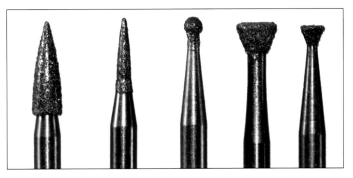

Diamond Bits

Diamond bits commonly have 3/32" and 1/8" diameter shafts (3/32" shafts were used herein) and come in a large variety of shapes and sizes in fine, medium, and coarse grits. The bit itself consists of the metal shaft and a metal head that has been encrusted with graded commercial diamond chips. For the most part, diamond bits will outlast ruby carvers, but are generally more expensive.

The diamond bits used for all the projects in this book consist of a set of five bits in three shapes that I use for all the small finish and detail shaping cuts that practically every animal carving requires. The aforementioned five are described as follows:

Flame 1/8" x 3/8" was used for heavier cutting required to prepare surfaces for the smaller flame. Any shaping and detailing cuts that require v-cuts, u-cuts, stock reduction, and/or undercutting.

Flame 1/16" x 1/4" was used for fine shaping and detailing, undercutting curls, hair splits, and ear/nostril detailing.

Ball 1/16" diameter was used for cutting nostrils, deepening ear hollows, grooves, and outlining.

Inverted Cone 1/8" diameter for coarse texturing, cutting V-grooves, and undercutting.

Inverted Cone 1/16" diameter for fine texturing, cutting V-grooves, and undercutting.

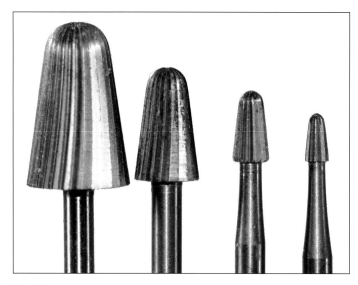

Steel Bits

The tapered steel bits used for the projects in this book are all single fluted bits with 3/32" shafts, and were used essentially for smoothing and shaping body contours, hair contours, and/or details that required a smoothness beyond what a ruby carver or diamond bit could give. The primary use for these bits is for outlining, shaping, and the shaping/smoothing of *feathers*, though not addressed within the scope of this book.

The bit heads were sized (5/16"D x 1/2"H), (3/16"D x 5/16"H), (1/8"D x 3/16"H), and (1/16"D x 1/8"H), and were used exclusively for outlining, shaping, and smoothing small, medium, and larger hair areas.

Texturing Bits

Stone Bits

All the stone bits used have 3/32" shafts and the head consisted of an admixture of ceramic and aluminum oxide particles. Depending on grit, these are fairly aggressive stone bits, but with a bit of practice, the carver will quickly be able to "read" their capabilities and use them to great advantage. The bit sizes and uses are listed as follows:

Cylinder Shape (3/16" x 5/8"), coarse grit, used for texturing large scale fur

Cylinder Shape (3/32" x 5/16"), fine grit, used for texturing small scale fur

Inverted Cone Shape (3/16" diameter), medium grit, used for texturing large scale fur

Inverted Cone Shape (1/8" diameter), fine grit, used for texturing small scale fur

Flame Shape (1/8" x 3/8"), medium grit, used for outlining, shaping, smoothing smaller detail, fur, or hair.

Ball Shape (1/8" diameter), fine grit, used for pre-texturing fur, grooving, and rounding out detail.

Smoothing/Sanding Bits

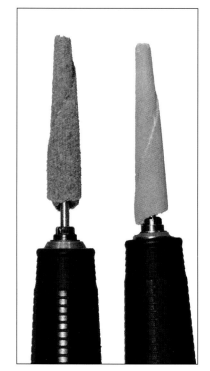

Tapered Sanding Mandrel

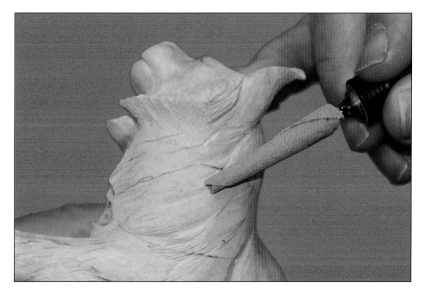

The tapered sanding mandrel featured here has a 3/32" shaft and is ideally suited for smaller smoothing operations, such as individual fur details, curls, and hair groups. This bit excels when used for general surface and shape smoothing on a smaller scale. I keep at least two, (usually three or four) tapered mandrels loaded with sandpaper grits ranging from 120 to 220 while addressing surface smoothing on woods such as Tupelo, Bass, & Walnut.

These bits are not made to run at high speeds and care should be taken not to use excessive speed. Due to the imbalance of the bit caused by spiral wrapping the sandpaper, extreme speeds can cause the shaft to bend. Optimum speed for any smoothing application should remain between 12,000 and 14,000 rpm (revolutions per minute).

This particular mandrel is by far the easiest and most forgiving of all sanding mandrels to use when addressing smaller details on any carving. Once an optimal speed is found to match a particular size of sanding grit, the smoothing process becomes an enjoyable task.

Please note – *nowhere* has it been mentioned that this bit should be used for **carving**. Thanks to maneuverability and ease of use, I find too many beginning students using the tapered mandrel to **shape** with, rather than *smooth* with – which more often than not results in misshapen details and/or complete removal thereof. Shapes should be established with carving bits, and those shapes should be honored while smoothing.

Loading the Tapered Sanding Mandrel

To successfully load the tapered sanding mandrel shown (3/32" shaft with a tapered 1" body) you must first cut the sandpaper to the pattern shown. Always use a **cloth-backed** sandpaper.

Before cutting the sandpaper to shape, first "break" the sandpaper by pulling it across the sharp corner of a table or bench with the back of the paper against the sharp table corner—pull first in one direction, and then another at a 90-degree angle. This will "soften" the sandpaper and allow it to roll onto the mandrel easier. For other woodworking applications, this process will also work on paper-backed sandpaper and allow a sheet to be evenly folded and cut or torn.

The tapered sanding mandrel is a very versatile tool to have in your arsenal of tool bits. When used properly, excellent results can be achieved while smoothing smaller variably contoured areas.

Proper use depends upon proper *speed* and proper *pressure* as applied to the surface being smoothed. Excess pressure will load the grit of the sanding taper and render the sanding surface useless – continued excessive pressure will create heat and then discoloration of the wood surface being smoothed, as well as devastation to the abrasive surface.

BEWARE! If you forget to set the rpm at a slow speed on a machine that generates 35,000 to 50,000 rpm, the inertia of high-speed rotation can bend the shaft! The mandrel is slightly out of balance due to the sandpaper wrap, and high-speed torque can bend the shaft, leaving you with a flail that is 5 to 6-inches in diameter revolving at many thousands of revolutions per minute. This not only stresses the handpiece motor, but the user while he or she tries desperately to shut the machine off.

If you are right-handed and therefore run your machine in the forward mode, cut and load the pattern appropriate to right-handed operation. If you are left-handed and run your machine in reverse as is common for left-handed users, cut and load the pattern appropriate to left-handed operation. Both left- and right-handed patterns are shown in the full-size pattern sketch shown below.

When cutting the abrasive cloth, the grit of the abrasive cloth should be against the **bottom** of the pattern with the "grit this side up" message on the top of the pattern visible.

Abrasive Cutting Pattern (shown actual size)

Right Handed Use Pattern
(Machine in Forward Rotation)

Left Handed Use Pattern
(Machine in Reverse Rotation)

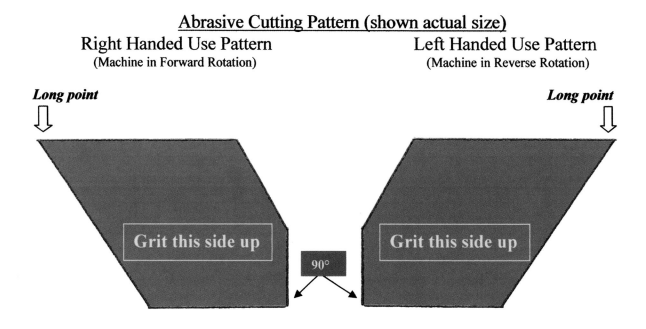

Long point

Grit this side up

90°

Long point

Grit this side up

Pattern: (See pattern sketch) Cut a pattern cutting template out of aluminum flashing, plastic, or laminate, and mark the grit side with *"grit this side up"* so there are no mistakes when cutting the pattern.

The following loading instructions are given for right-handed use.

1. Always use cloth-backed abrasive – paper backed abrasive doesn't mount on the mandrel as well and quickly deteriorates.

2. Cut pattern (with the grit the proper side up) with an old pair of scissors.

3. Holding the sandpaper in the left hand with right-angled corner on the lower right-hand side and the mandrel held in the right hand, insert the right angle corner evenly into the slot of the mandrel.

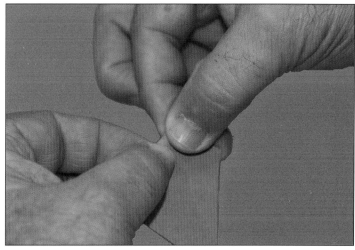

4. Tightly pinching the abrasive with both thumbs and forefingers, Begin rolling the sandpaper tightly on the sloped body of the mandrel, while exerting most of the pressure on the tip of the roll with the fingers of the left hand.

5. Continue rolling sandpaper until the entire pattern is rolled and the narrow point of the sandpaper pattern terminates about even with the bottom or largest diameter of the mandrel body. If it doesn't, unwrap the abrasive and cock the edge in the slot (forward or backwards) slightly to bring the point back to the base of the roll on the mandrel once it is re-rolled.

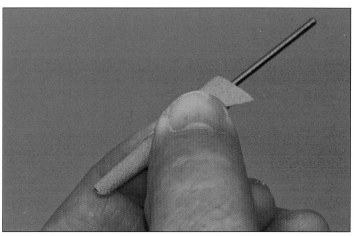

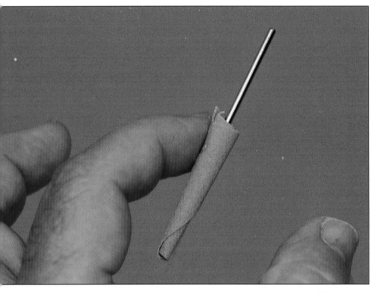

6. Place one drop (be frugal!) of "super glue" under the end of the narrow point and hold without moving until glue has set. (Usually 15 to 30 seconds)

7. Try **not** to allow any superglue to seep out from under the abrasive cloth and stick your fingers.

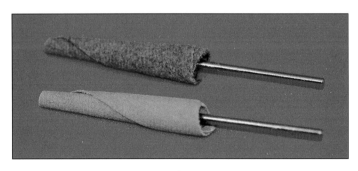

8. Once you achieve the technique for loading the mandrel, load at least two mandrels – one with fine and one with coarse gritted cloth so you can go from coarse sanding to finish sanding without having to reload a mandrel.

9. A final reminder, while sanding, sand with the machine running at a slower RPM (revolutions per minute) – with a micromotor machine such as the one shown, 12,000 to 15,000 RPM is usually sufficient for continued sanding without clogging the sandpaper grit or worse, bending the shaft of the mandrel.

Medium and Large Cylindrical Sanding Mandrels

Both of these sanding mandrels come with pattern templates (usually metal) that are used to cut the sandpaper to size. The ends of the sandpaper are inserted into a holding slot as the paper is slid on over the body of the mandrel. As a rule, the sandpaper is then tightened onto the mandrel by use of an inner elongated tube that is turned into place with an "L" shaped tool that exerts proper pressure on the ends of the sandpaper to hold it in place during use.

The small cylinder sanding mandrel has a 1/4" shaft and the cylinder measures roughly 1/2" x 2". It is used to smooth intermediate shapes, contours, and surfaces.

The large cylinder sanding mandrel also has a 1/4" shaft, but the cylinder measures 3/4" x 3" and is used for smoothing larger shapes, contours, and surfaces.

Cleaning Bits

Rotary Brush

The best rotary brushes with which to clean carving detail and texturing surfaces are those with softer white bristled brush heads. With a foot-controlled handpiece, I can regulate the "stiffness" of the softer bristled brushes without destroying any of the finely textured surface detail, as can happen if a very stiff, coarse bristled brush is used.

The roughing bits featured throughout this book were provided by:

L.R.Oliver & Co, Inc.
7445 Mayer Road
Cottrellville, Michigan 48039
www.olivercorp.com

Other bits (with exception of the sanding cylinders) were provided by:

The Foredom Electric Co
16 Stony Hill Road
Bethel, Connecticut 06801-1029
www.foredom.com

Rotary brushes are available in 3/32", 1/8", and 1/4", with brush diameters ranging from 1 inch up to 3 or 4 inches or more, and are used to clean textured surfaces of a carving prior to applying sealer and finishes. I find the 2 to 3 inch diameter brush optimal for cleaning carvings.

Safety

Improper handling of the carving machines illustrated in this book can certainly result in a nasty cut or grind mark on your hands, arms, or legs (should you drop the handpiece in your lap). But for the most part, I would not consider these life threatening. What is extremely life threatening, with prolonged practice, is the inhalation of the fine dust created by the carving process, whether roughing, shaping, sanding, or texturing.

As carvers, we usually take time to keep our work area clean of the wood dust, shavings, and other debris generated by the wasting away process connected with the carving project. Unfortunately, we often fail to deal with what is most dangerous to our health, that being the air-laden particles of wood dust that we can't see, and readily inhale without proper protection.

Please take every precaution to protect yourself against breathing these floating particles. Provide your workstation and work area with proper ventilation and a collection device that removes them from around your face and the space from which you breath. I use the combination of a dust collector and dust mask while I work. I also have a filtered air purifier suspended from the ceiling in my work area that further cleans the air as I work.

During the course of my carving career, I have had to receive medical attention no less than four times due to respiratory problems created by my casual and ignorant approach to dust control. I believe I have finally learned the value of the so-called "ounce of prevention" – I haven't had an attempt made to plunge a lung biopsy needle into my chest for years!

Eye Shape and Location

Be aware not only of placement of the eyes on the head of the animal you are carving, but of shape.

The eyes of a prey species such as a rabbit or a deer, are proportionately larger and more rounded than the eyes of predators like wolves, foxes, and cats, whose eyes appear smaller, elongated, and more triangulated.

The eyes of prey species are located more to the side of the head, allowing for a greater field of vision, whereas the eyes of predator species are located more forward on the head with a more directional field of vision.

Glass Eyes

I prefer setting glass eyes in my carvings of animals, especially for cane heads, because I feel it gives the carving as well as the cane a more realistic, finished, and attractive look. For example, I like the looks of a lion cane head carved from black walnut with yellow/brown glass eyes. The whole cane head seems to come alive because more realism can be given to a carving with glass eyes and modeled eyelids, than can be given to a carved eye, with much less time and effort. Glass eyes are preferred for several reasons, but the primary reasons are realism and ease of setting. Other reasons include uniformity of size and roundness, color, and shine.

There are many carvers who would prefer to carve eyes rather than set glass eyes and for them I have included a section on carving eyes (see *Carving Eyes*).

Setting Glass Eyes

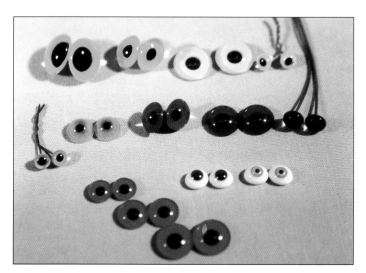

1. Select proper size and color of eyes for the project.

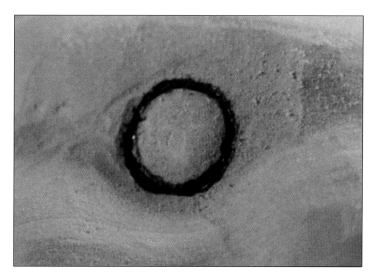

2. Ensure that the eye locations are perfectly drawn from side to side, and that they are symmetrical and uniform when viewed from the front, top, and sides. Nothing will ruin the appearance of the carving more than eyes that are miss-located by having one eye higher than the other, or one further back on the head than the other. It is imperative that the surface immediately around the eye be relieved enough to allow the eye to be inserted and plumb. (The flat back of the eye must be straight up and down as opposed to being tilted in or out.) Take the time to check position from all possible directions, and adjust as necessary. This is the step to correct any imperfections, rather than try to adjust later on.

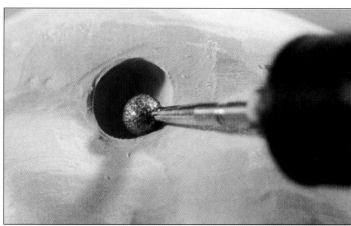

3. Using a ball shaped bit, touch the bit to the center of the eye location, and begin applying pressure without letting the bit wander. Using a slight circular motion, begin shaping the eyehole until the shape of the hole is of the proper depth and diameter to fit the eye. As you approach the size of the eye, keep fitting the eye to the hole until the eye will slide into the hole.

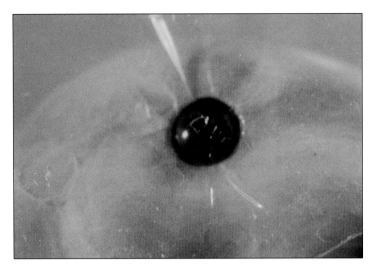

4. Leave the eyes in a plastic bag and fit an eye to the hole through the bag. When the eye and the thickness of the bag will enter the hole, the hole is of proper size.

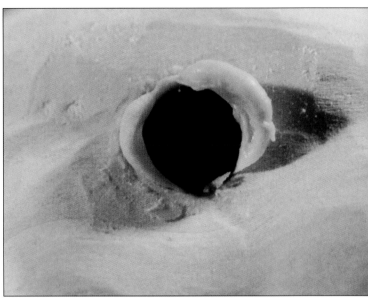

7. Push the eye into the eye cavity with the hollowed end of dowel modeling tool until the eye protrudes out of the head to the desired amount. *Note: A general rule of thumb is to allow the eye to extend out of the head approximately one-third of the eye diameter.* Make sure the eye is plumb with respect to the subject's head. An easy way to check this is to think of the back of the eye as a flat plain and make sure that the flat is straight up and down and not tilted outward or inward within the eye cavity.

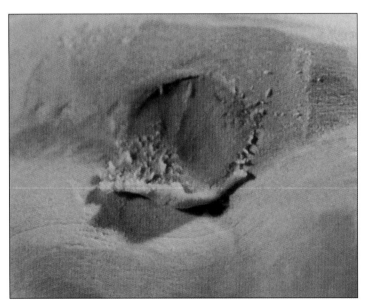

5. Fill the eye cavity with two part epoxy putty and level to the edges of the cavity.

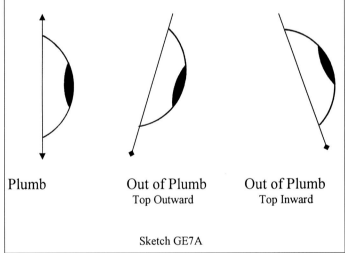

Plumb   Out of Plumb   Out of Plumb
                  Top Outward   Top Inward

Sketch GE7A

6. Before you start the glass eye installation, you should have a modeling tool with which to properly position the eye as it is being pushed into the eye cavity, remove excess epoxy, to model the shape of the eye, and to model and texture the eyelids. The simplest and most effective tool is a 1/4-inch dowel that has been sharply tapered at one end and semi-sharpened with a concave indentation at the other.

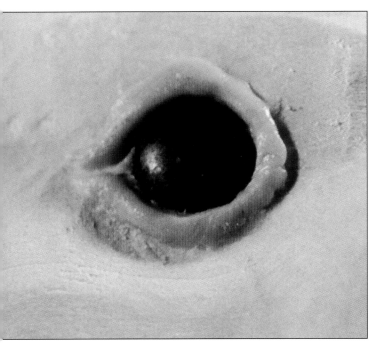

8. Remove excess epoxy putty that is pushed out of cavity as the eye displaces it, and model eyelid of the type that is suitable to the type of animal being carved. *Hint** Gather whatever reference photos you can of the eye area of the animal that you are carving.

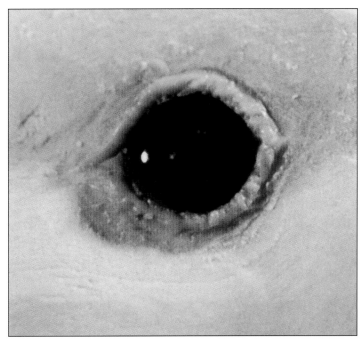

10. After the epoxy has set, clean any film and/or residue off the eye by rubbing the tip of the modeling tool around and around on the surface of the eye, within the eyelids. This will make the eye shiny and unblemished, as it should be.

Carving Eyes

Due to ease of installation, preference is usually given to setting *glass* eyes on carvings – I'm sure a lot of caricature carvers would give me argument on this – and on functional carvings such as cane heads or walking sticks, some carvers prefer to carve the eyes rather than setting glass eyes. Glass eyes are preferred for the vast majority of bird and animal carvings, but some carvers prefer the carved effect throughout their carvings – to this end I include an eye carving sequence.

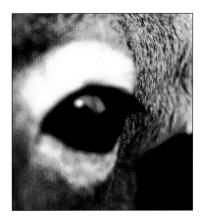

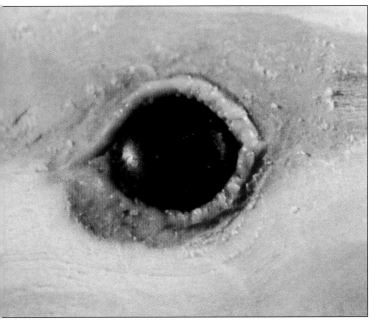

9. Touch up each eye to assure that the eyes match as closely as possible. Do not handle the carving until epoxy putty has thoroughly hardened. *Note: In order to ascertain that the modeled epoxy around the eye has hardened, make a small ball of leftover epoxy from the same batch as used on the eye and test it from time to time to see when proper hardness is achieved.*

As with any project, surround yourself with as much reference material as possible to supply every aspect of detail needed to carve the eye of the subject. This applies not only to eyes, but also to every detail of the animal, whether it be the shape of eyes, nose, ears, mouth, ... right down to finished fur detail.

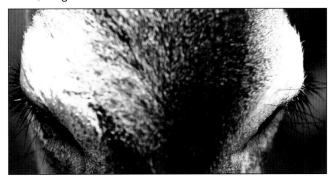

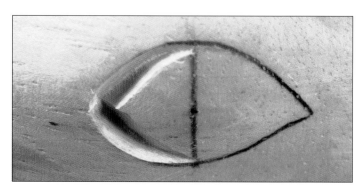

Make a second cut starting with the same point as the first cut in the corner of the eye, and draw along the lower eyelid upwards to the control line in the same manner as the first cut. This second cut will match the first cut.

Once I determine the size, shape, and detail of the eye, I will often sketch it on a sheet of paper to totally familiarize myself with the details I will be carving.

Carefully prepare the mound or raised portion into which the eye will be carved. Make sure the eye mounds are of a suitable mass to receive the size of eye you wish to carve, but because of their mass, they are not out of proportion with the rest of the head. Once both eye mounds are as symmetrical as possible, smooth the contour in preparation to draw the eye in place.

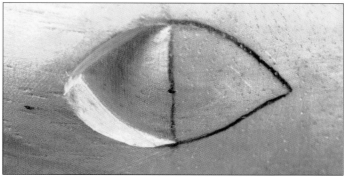

Remove the stock between the two cuts from the corner of the eye to the control line evenly from side to side, using the side of the flame shaped bit. The area removed with resemble a triangular wedge shape.

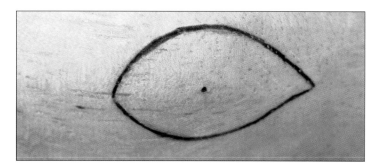

Lay out the shape of the eye as accurately as possible on both sides. I use dividers to locate the center of each eye from a common point on the head (usually the tip of the nose). If the eyes don't appear uniformly placed once they are drawn, it is usually indicative that too much or too little stock has been left on one side or the other, and must be corrected by removing a bit more stock from the side that appears to have more stock.

Repeat the same cuts on the opposite corner of the eye – the eye now has two triangular facets with a sharp ridge running vertically through the middle.

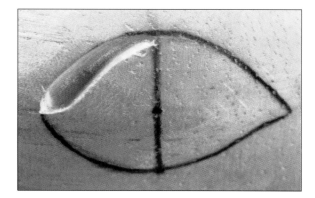

Draw a control line vertically through the center of each eye, lid to lid. Using a flame shaped diamond bit or ruby carver of appropriate size to the eye being carved, make the first cut. Beginning at one corner of the eye, cut deeply with the tip of the bit, then draw along the upper eyelid to the control line – this cut becomes shallower until it runs out at the control line.

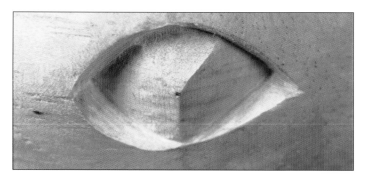

Beginning at the exact center of the vertical ridge, remove a triangular wedge of stock that gets deeper as it runs to the upper eyelid.

Starting at the same center point of the vertical ridge, remove another triangular wedge that gets slightly deeper as it runs to the lower eyelid. The "eyeball" now has a very angular appearance and the faceted look of a pyramid.

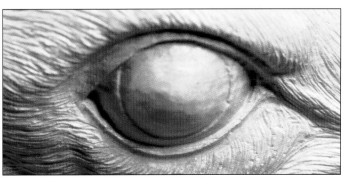

17. Prepare the area around the eyes for texturing by drawing texture lines, then carefully texturing the fur around the eye with an inverted cone shaped or cylinder shaped texturing bit.

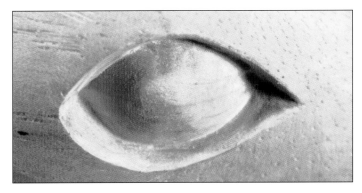

Round out the eyeball from the pyramid shape, keeping within the eyelids. Remember the eyeball is spherical, while the eyelids and contours around the eyelids are more oval in appearance.

Sharpen up any areas and details within the eye that need defining.

Define any lines and indentations that lead outwards from the corners of the eyes.

If the animal has a lid fold above the eye, carve it in, and blend it into the surrounding area.

If the animal has a raised area below the eye and/or details like the preorbital gland on a deer, shape and blend into surrounding area.

Painting an Animal Eye

The size of the eye will determine to some extent whether you choose to use an airbrush or a manual brush – depending on your choice and skill with either one. If the eye is tiny, the fine point of a round brush is usually sufficient for each step required to color the entire eye. I have used an airbrush for so long that I prefer to lay color with it whenever possible, then finish with a fine pointed manual brush anything these shaky old hands can't accomplish with an airbrush.

Whatever the choice to apply color, what follows is the sequence and method of color application that I use.

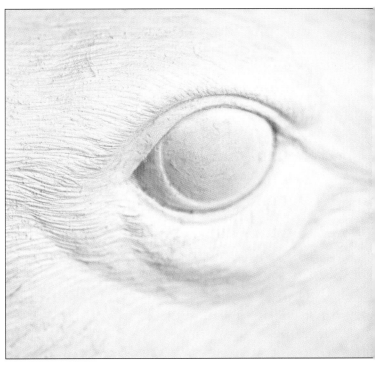

Seal the area of the eye with flat lacquer cut with lacquer thinner – if you are painting the entire carving, this would be the point where you seal and gesso the entire carving. The ratio for the sealing application is 50/50 (50 percent lacquer to 50 percent lacquer thinner). Once you have sealed the eye area and/or carving, gesso the areas to be painted with several coats of thinned gesso.

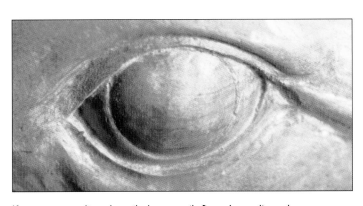

If you want a relieved pupil, draw pupils first, then relieve them away with an appropriately sized ball shaped bit. Make absolutely certain that the size and location of the pupils are the same on both eyes. You can spoil the overall appearance of the carving at this point. *Note: Also be aware of the different pupil shapes on different animals, some have round, some are elongated, and some, like cats and foxes can have pointed ovals or spherical shapes.*

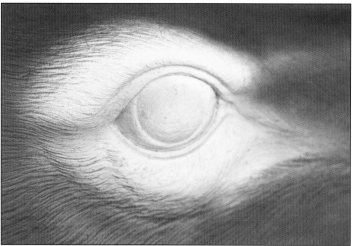

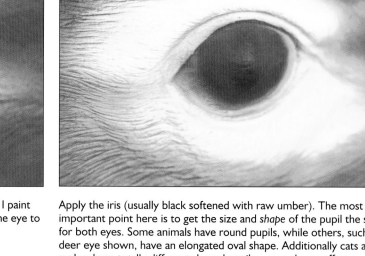

I prefer to have the areas around the eyes finish painted before I paint the eyes, because it is easier for me to stay within the area of the eye to paint rather than try to paint around the eye after it is painted.

Apply the iris (usually black softened with raw umber). The most important point here is to get the size and *shape* of the pupil the same for both eyes. Some animals have round pupils, while others, such as the deer eye shown, have an elongated oval shape. Additionally cats and snakes have totally different shaped pupils – so make an effort to familiarize yourself as much with the details of eyes of the subject animal you carve as well as the details of the rest of the head and body.

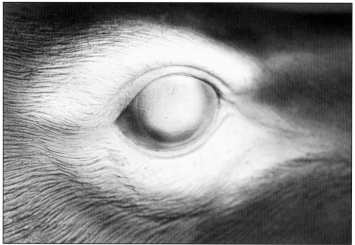

Next, give attention to the area considered the "white" of the eye. I find most animals have very little white exposure to the eye with exception of around the very edges of the eye, as is the case with the deer eye that I am painting for coloring this sequence. What would be considered the white of the eye on a human has much less exposure on animals…unless they are frightened – then the white is very evident. Watch a horse or rabbit that is frightened and as the eyes open wider in fright, much more white is exposed.

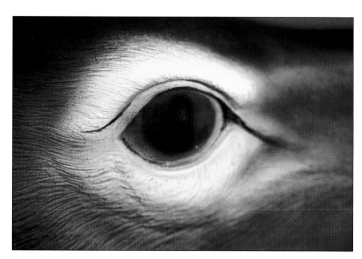

Paint in the shadow and minutely detailed areas around the eye. This eye was painted entirely with an airbrush until I got to the finite hairline accents where I had to use a very fine point round sable brush.

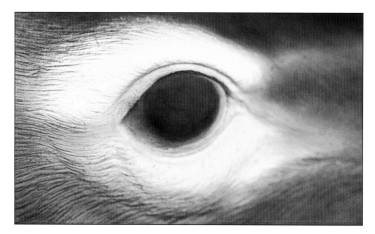

Paint the area of the pupil with the color applicable to the animal you have carved. Detail in this area will depend primarily on the size of the eye that has been carved. Some animals appear to have an almost solid color to the pupil, while others have a striated pattern. The size of the pupil dilation will also determine how much of the iris color is exposed.

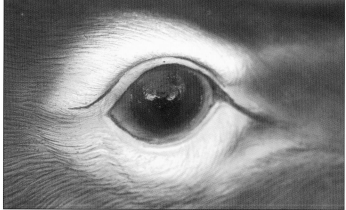

Once all painted areas are dry, to give the eye a realistically wet appearance, I cover the portion of the eye within the lids with straight gloss lacquer.

Fur

Fur Contour & Detail

For the most part, all the fur textured on the projects in this book will be stone textured (as opposed to being textured with a wood burner) for two reasons. First, I feel stone texturing gives a softer, more realistic appearance to an animal carving. Secondly, for me, stone texturing is easier to manipulate (curls, separations, and overlays), easier to apply, faster, and far less tiring with regard to hand fatigue and effort.

For the above considerations, I prefer to create fur contour and detail by relieving/shaping with a flame-shape diamond or ruby carver, and then texturing with a stone bit, which as previously mentioned, gives fur a softer look. If necessary, though quite infrequently, I accentuate various fur detailing with a skew or spear point wood burning pen, but as a rule I can accomplish finite cuts and accentuating depressions with a very small flame shaped diamond bit.

Before texturing begins, it is imperative that all final shape contours to be textured are finish shaped, smoothed, and detailed to accept texturing. Details will include such particulars as separations between grouped hairs, curls, hair overlays, and undercuts.

Some texturing guidelines:
• Always texture from the bottom to the top.
• Always texture from the rear forward.
• Use random length strokes
• Always follow your drawn flow lines.
• Use a depth of stroke and length of stroke appropriate to the hair size of the animal being carved.
• Use undulating lines of strokes
• Overlap previous row of strokes by about one-third stroke length.
• For continuity, periodically run a longer texture stroke over and through a couple of previously textured rows.
• Be aware of how the fur lays and/or "flows" on the animal you are carving. The fact that your carving is beautifully textured doesn't help if the texturing is applied in a wrong direction or with a wrong pattern.
• Cause fur to gracefully change direction or to transition from one side of the carving to the other. All too often, a carving will show evidence of its carver's inability to gracefully change directions from side to side – as evidenced by the sides coming together along the backbone in the shape of "V's" where the fur meets from one side to the other. When this is done repeatedly, the V's join together to form what the observer will perceive as miniature textured "Christmas Trees" along the back, on the neck, the

head, and even on the legs of the carving…something never found on a real animal. To accomplish a transition or direction change, as an example: bring a left-handed stroke up to a point just short of becoming a right-handed stroke. Before beginning or blending into the right-handed strokes, fill an area between the change with several straight strokes which gradually bend and work into the beginning (or ending) of right-hand strokes.

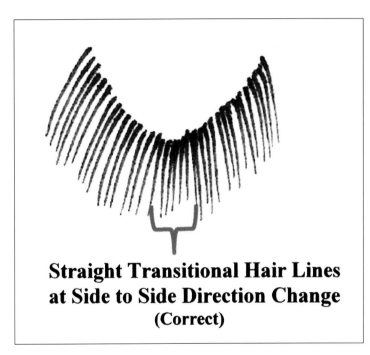

Straight Transitional Hair Lines at Side to Side Direction Change
(Correct)

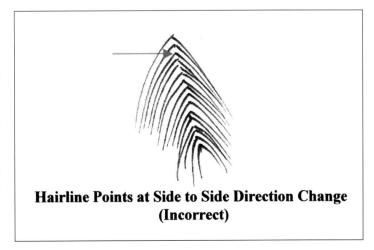

Hairline Points at Side to Side Direction Change
(Incorrect)

Texturing Fur and Hair
with a Stone Bit

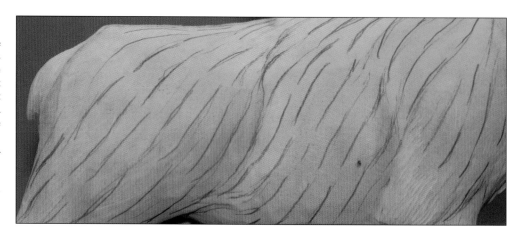

1. Draw hair or fur "flow lines" over the entire carving. These drawn flow lines will foretell quite accurately how the finished textured carving will look. At this point, I always hold the carving at arm's length, or observe it from a distance to see that the lines I have drawn are in a direction and a "pattern" that will add quality, realism, and a pleasing appearance to the carving. If I don't care for what I see, I erase all areas that I dislike and redraw the lines until I am satisfied with what I observe.

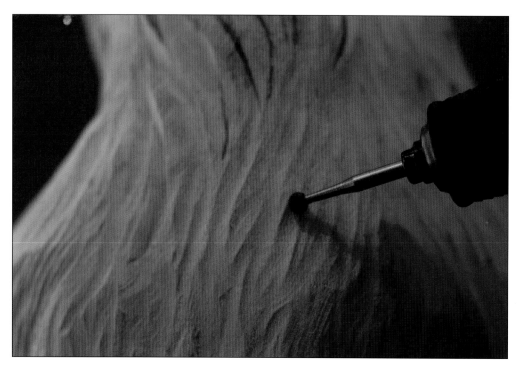

2. Pre-texturing – often, if you wish to give the impression of soft coarse hair, it is advantageous to accentuate the drawn hair pattern with a stone or fine diamond ball bit to create larger grooves, ridges, and deeper depths to the surface of the area to be textured prior to texturing. Pre-texturing with a ball in this manner often gives the fur a softer, fuller, and more realistic look after final texturing. It takes extra time, but on some carvings, the extra time and effort is worth it. By following the flow lines, indentations are made with the pre-texturing ball bit that can be followed with the texturing inverted cone bit.

3. Texture fur following the suggestions mentioned above. Use an inverted cone or cylinder shaped stone bit of appropriate fur scale/size to the size of the carved subject. Follow in the direction dictated by the pre-texturing lines or the penciled flow lines. *Rule: Always texture from the rear forward, and from the bottom to the top—this will give a natural appearance of hair where the upper hairs lay over the bottom hairs (shingled in a manner that allows water to drained down and off the animal.*

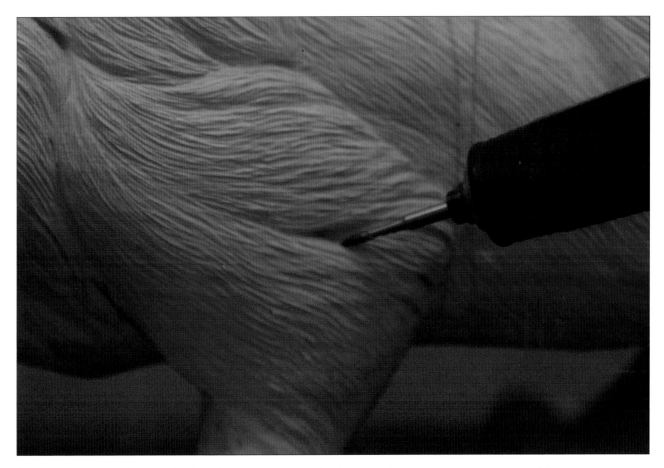

4. Upon completion of the texturing, look the carving over completely to see where you can accentuate areas of the fur by deepening "V" shaped separations or slots.
• A small flame shaped diamond bit is used by plunging the tip of the bit, then drag stroking outward while still honoring the textured fur beside it. You may have to go back and touch up where you remove textured fur.

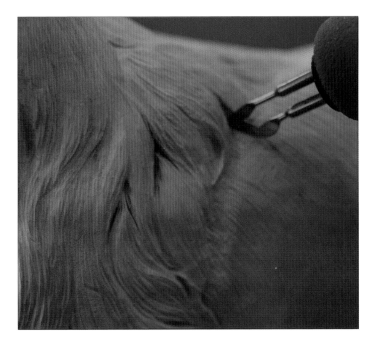

• Another method of accentuating is to use a skew tipped burning pen with a medium to light heat to deepen the lines of fur in existing "v" shaped hair separations and elongated slots.

5. When all areas and directions of fur are completely textured, clean the entire area with a rotary brush run at a slow to medium speed. It is imperative that the texturing debris be removed from the textured area. If a rotary brush is not available, use an old toothbrush and scrub the textured feathers clean. Any tiny particles left on the carving from the texturing operation will be locked on the surface when the carving is sealed in preparation for the final finish, so be thorough with the cleaning process.

Carving Details

Carving a Green Limb Cane

Any tree that falls through natural or intended reason around my house, gets a careful inspection to see whether it has a limb or limbs with suitable configuration to make a cane. Thanks to the folks that heat their homes with wood, I can usually expect a goodly supply of green cane blanks whenever family or neighbors are out cutting wood for winter fuel.

2. Cut the limb longer than required for a cane shaft, and cut enough of the trunk above and below the joint of the limb to satisfy the shape and size of the handle you wish to carve.

1. Select a tree with a limb that grows as parallel with the trunk as possible and is of a size that will satisfy a cane shaft.

3. With a chainsaw, carefully cut a slab from the trunk to satisfy the width of the handle you wish to carve. Choose a direction off the limb joint for the slab that will best suit the way the limb joins the trunk, will best fit your pattern, and will provide the strongest, most attractive grain pattern for the handle.

4. A slabbed trunk and limb section ready to receive pattern outlines.

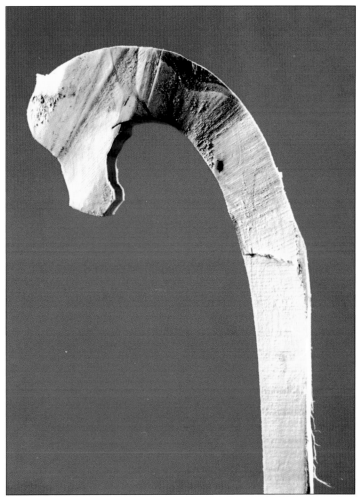

6. Cut the pattern outline (side view) with a band saw. There are times when cutting the top view is also possible on the band saw, as is shown. Usually, however, the blank shaft (limb portion) gets in the way and prevents accurate cutting. If this is the case, remove stock for the top view to desired thickness and then shape by hand. With the blank shown, the limb shaft was far to large to use, so I cut it down to a manageable squared sized that will be later rounded by rounding the corners with a router, then sanding to a uniform roundness.

5. Orient the pattern on the trunk slab in a manner that will best bring the pattern lines to the limb. The pattern used for this blank was the saddle horse pattern featured in this book.

7. Lay out rough details and contours of the head

41

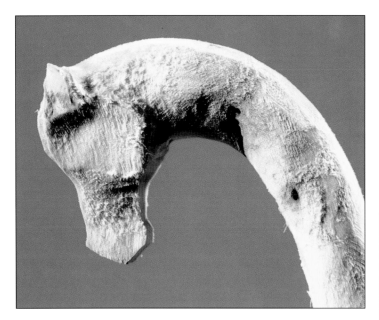

8. Rough shape head to remove as much excess wood as possible before stabilizing the green wood in the next step.

10. Stabilized limb & trunk cane blank with penciled contours, ready to carve. After the cane blank handle has soaked in wood stabilizer for twenty-four hours, I wipe it dry, then wash the entire area with lacquer thinner, and allow the blank to dry for another twenty-four hours.

9. Since the blank was taken from a newly cut tree (red maple) and was "green" enough to contain a goodly amount of sap, to prevent checking or splitting, the thicker handle portion was soaked in Pentacryl® for twenty-four hours to stabilize the grain structure. Pentacryl will completely penetrate a carving blank this size in a twenty-four-hour period. (see Pentacryl definition and specifications below). To prevent the cane shaft from checking or splitting, I apply one or two coats of Pentacryl to the shaft with a brush. A sparse coating is sufficient to stabilize anything having the thickness of a cane shaft.

11. Rough carved and smoothed limb/trunk blank ready for finish detailing, texturing, and setting of eyes.
12. Add details, texturing, and eyes as per instructions found in Texturing with a Stone Bit on page 37, and Setting Glass Eyes on page 31.

Pentacryl Defined

Pentacryl was originally developed for the treatment of waterlogged wood, but has since become an invaluable source to keep green wood from cracking, checking, and/or splitting for woodcarvers, woodturners, and woodworkers. Pentacryl is a compound of siliconized polymers that does not discolor wood, is non-hydroscopic (does not gather moisture), and will not oxidize, decompose, or migrate in wood when exposed to different degrees of temperature and/or relative humidity.

Pentacryl can be applied by brush, spraying, or soaking. I find soaking to be the most beneficial, not only with regard to penetration, but to time, in that I can put several green and freshly cut cane blanks in a container of the fluid at once, and go on to other things while waiting for it to penetrate. Incidentally, wood does not have to be completely saturated with the liquid to be stabilized.

Wood treated with pentacryl will accept most finishes, whether acrylic or oil based. The key to success with *any* application of finish is that the Pentacryl surface be as dry as possible. Stain added to Pentacryl will color a carving blank while it stabilizes the wood structure. The depth of color obtained depends on the amount of stain added.

Technical data, specifications, and retailer listings can be obtained from their website at: www.preservation-solutions.com or

Preservation Solutions
1060 Bunker Hill Road
Jefferson, Maine 04348

Speaking of cutting natural walking sticks – if you don't own the property where you have located saplings such as this, it would be a good idea to get permission from the land-owner to cut one or two before you "cut and run," so to speak! I was headed across a property that I had permission to deer hunt on – although this time armed with a shovel and axe, when the caretaker drove out and asked where I was going with the tools. I explained what I intended to do, and he explained what I was NOT going to do until we checked with the owner, and the venture ended for that day!

Carving the African Elephant Walking Stick Head

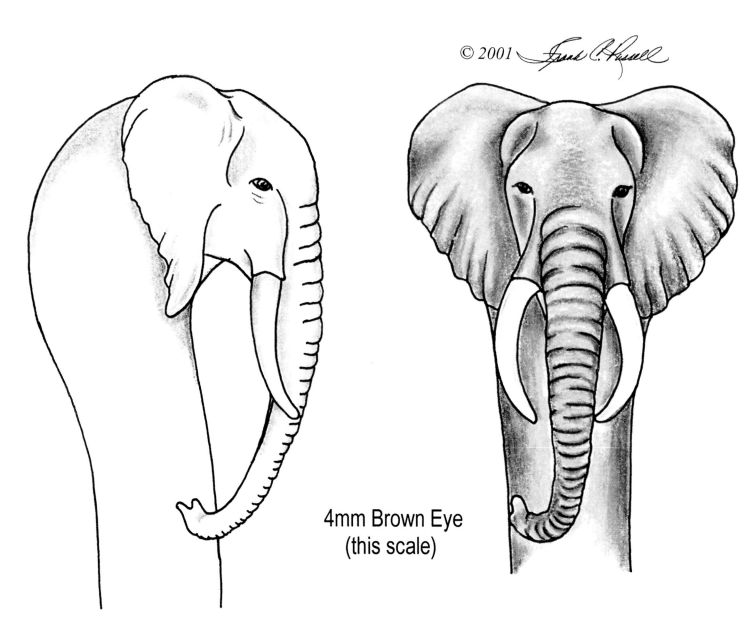

4mm Brown Eye
(this scale)

Before beginning *any* carving project, there is a planning procedure that we have to follow to avoid delay, wasted time, and/or error during the carving process.

First, we must ensure that we have a comfortable and safe working environment with machinery in working order.

Secondly, we need to be certain that we have selected the proper bits and accessories to accomplish the carving sequence in an appropriate (and enjoyable) manner.

Thirdly, and as important as the first and second steps of our planning, we must acquire knowledge of the subject. First-hand knowledge of a living subject is best, supplemented by reference drawings and photos. The point to this third stage is that *you can't carve what you don't know* – so surround yourself with references that will be useful to you and pay attention to them all through the carving process.

Firsthand photos, books, magazines, detail drawings, taxidermy mounts, or any combination thereof will help you achieve the detail you need to produce a quality carving. The references I used to carve the following elephant project, I got from photos taken years ago at a Florida zoo, several books, and recent references and photos I found on the internet – all because I have yet to observe, first hand, an elephant in the mountains of my Vermont home where I write this…

For the rabbit project shown later, I actually started with a road-kill I found while out fishing one day. That road-kill, plus other rabbit photos I had in my reference library, was sufficient to allow me to draw the two rabbit patterns found in the pattern section of this book.

Preparing the Carving Block

Whenever possible, transfer the pattern to the carving stock to reflect both the side view and the top view. Any shape, size, and detail presented by the outlines of both views will lend accuracy to the sawn blank and greatly benefit in the carving sequences. Make sure that both pattern views are registered properly from top to bottom and from side to side.

Always begin a cane project such as this with an *accurately squared* block of stock. Cut the block to a size that will fit the pattern you have selected with just a bit to spare. A squared block is necessary to accurately drill a hole to receive the shaft, or to receive whatever cane connecting hardware you choose.

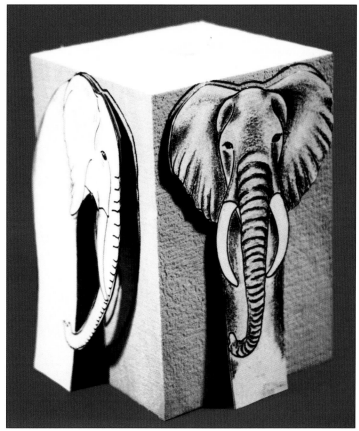

2. Transfer the outline of the side and top views of the pattern to the carving block by drawing around the patterns with a pencil.

3. Make sure the top view and the side view are registered accurately one to the other. This is necessary for two reasons – first, to accurately saw the carving blank, and, second, to accurately locate and drill the receiving hole for the shaft or cane hardware.

1. Make a template by gluing the front and side pattern views to a piece of poster board or sheet plastic and carefully cutting them out. I prefer this method because I can use the pattern template over and over again. Some carvers just make an extra copy of the pattern, cut out the outline, glue the views to the block using a glue stick, and then cut around the glued outline. This works if you don't plan to carve the same piece again. I prefer to keep the template patterns to use again or to share with students and carving friends.

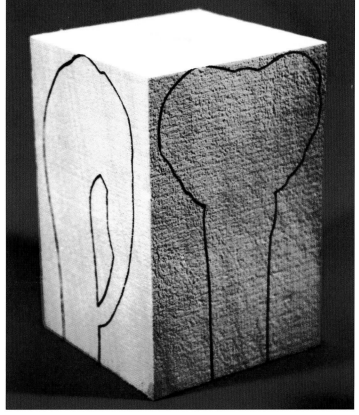

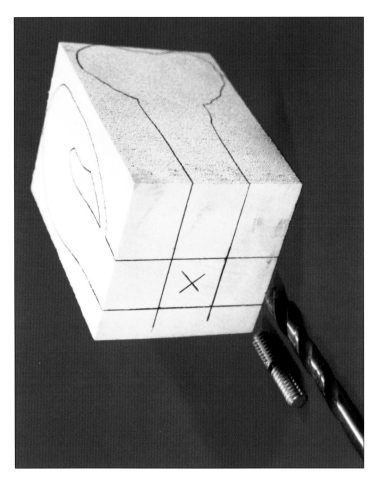

4. From the front and side views, transfer the thickness of the neck across the bottom of the carving block. Carefully measure and mark the centers along the length and width of the thickness of the neck. This center can be best located by carefully drawing diagonal lines from corner to corner – the center point is accurately located where they cross.

   Choose the size of drill bit to drill the receiving hole that will receive the cane shaft or cane hardware.

1. Cut the first view (as a rule, the side view is best to begin cutting with, but I chose to cut the front view first for clarification). Leave the sides or front and rear of the carving block intact. *This not only preserves the outline of the front view for cutting, but also leaves support under the blank as the remaining view is being cut.*

2. Put the sawn pieces back together and wrap a piece of masking tape around the entire assembly.

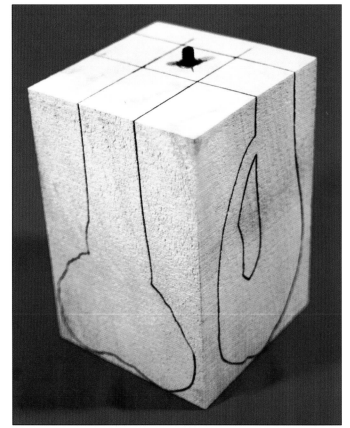

5. Carefully register the drill on the center point of the receiving hole, drill the hole, and fit the type of cane hardware that has been chosen to the hole. *Note: It is usually best **not** to glue the cane hardware in place until you are satisfied with the progress of the nearly completed carving.*

3. Saw the remaining view (in this case, the side view) leaving a portion of the masking tape to hold the pieces together where the tape has been wrapped across the pattern outline.

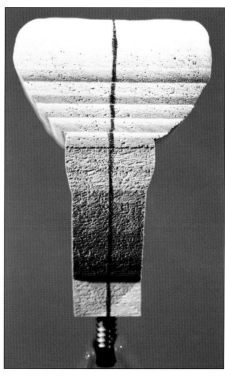

1. Draw a centerline all around the carving, beginning at a point on the front, then up over the head, down the center of the back of the neck and back to the point of beginning. Whenever the carving process removes the centerline, replace it, as it is extremely important to maintain symmetry while carving.

4. Holding the blank with fingers away from the saw blade, finish cutting through the masking tape on both sides of the front view. Discard waste pieces.

Rough Carving the Blank

When roughing out, always be aware of the amount of stock that you are removing – leaving a little excess stock is always a safer means to work. You can always remove stock as you go – it is difficult to replace if you remove too much.

As the head is being rounded out, make every effort to achieve a symmetrical roundness without any flat areas and without any squarish corners. The major mark of a beginner is a squarish looking carving, primarily due to the fear of removing too much stock. Study the subject through reference photos, videos, or if possible, in the flesh, to ascertain the natural shape (and grace) of even an animal as large as an elephant or walrus.

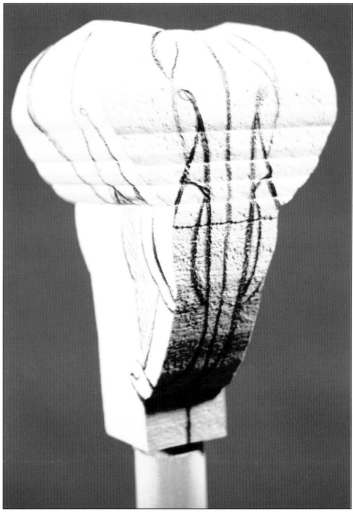

2. Draw all the detail control lines for the contours and major details of the head. Give particular attention to the trunk, tusks, forehead, eye mounds, and the jaw as it runs from under and between the tusks. Draw the general shape of the hollows and folds of the ears and the area where they join the head.

3. Draw a circle on the base of the carving that will match the size of the cane or walking stick shaft that will be adjoined to it. Note: I purchased regular washers with every size of outside diameter that I thought would match the different sizes of shafts and cane heads I would ever carve. Where necessary, I drilled the centers to fit over the cane joinery hardware so that I can slip the appropriate sized washer over the protruding hardware and draw around it, giving me a perfectly round circle to carve to.

4. Using a medium sized flame shaped carbide bit, round the top of the head down the back of the neck, and around the bottom of the neck.

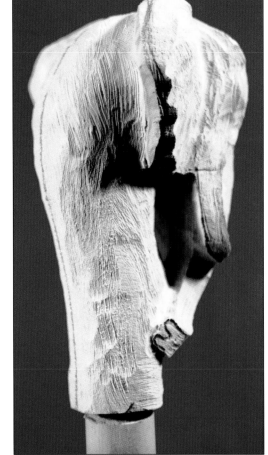

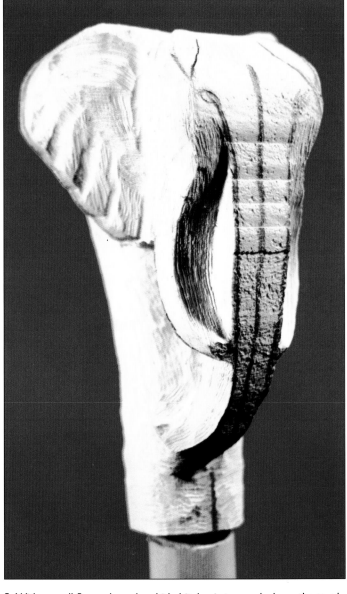

5. With a small flame shaped carbide bit, begin to rough shape the trunk, tusks, ears, lower jaw, and front of the head. Leaving shapes such as the trunk, tusks, and sides of the head squared at this point will be very helpful when it comes to carving for finished size and symmetry.

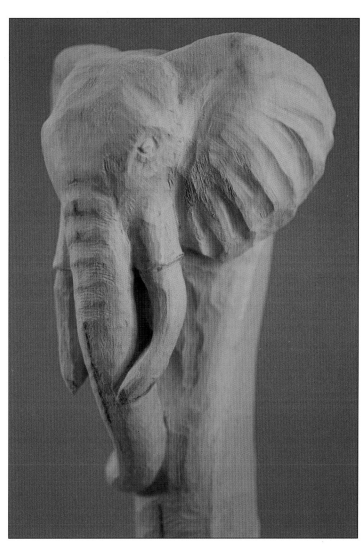

8. Lightly sand with a tapered mandrel to remove rough spots in preparation for refining and finishing detail.

6. Replace centerline and area control lines as were drawn in step two.

7. Round out and rough contour major shapes such as the neck, head, tusks, trunk, and ears.

    Check symmetry of entire head. With a large flame shaped ruby carver, lightly remove stock as necessary to bring entire head to desired size and contour shape.

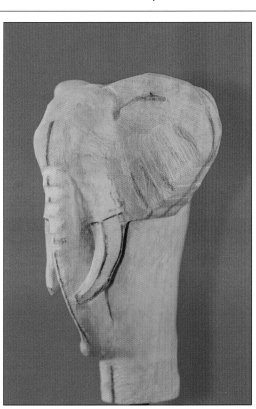

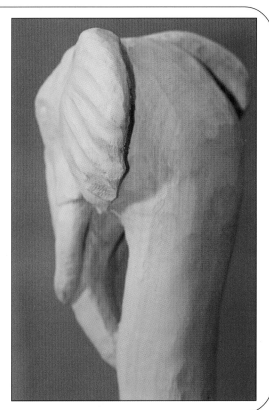

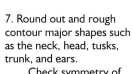

49

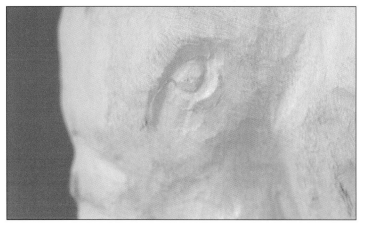

9. Prepare the eye areas for your choice of eye –

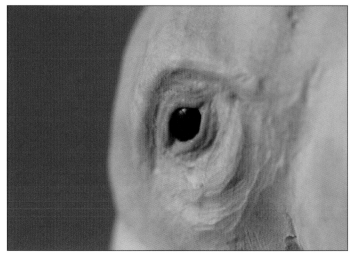

10. Set eyes as described in the "Setting Glass Eyes" section on page 31. Glass eyes were chosen for this project because I feel glass eyes give the finished carving a better look for a cane or walking stick head project.

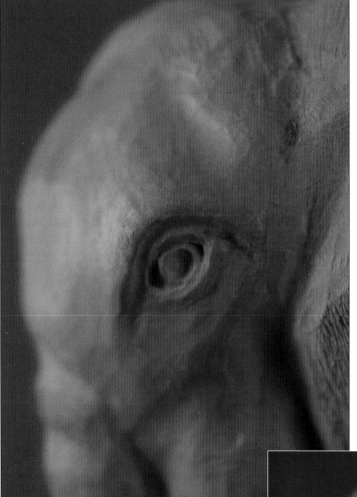

• If carved eyes are preferred, carve the eyes as described in the "Carved Eyes" section on page 33.

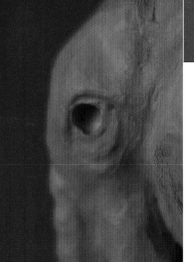

• If glass eyes are preferred, cut in the eye cavities with a small ball shaped diamond or ruby carver in preparation to setting eyes.

11. With the eyes in place, the elephant head is now ready for finish carving and detailing.

Finish Carving and/or Detailing

Bring all aspects of the head to a smoothed and finished shape in preparation for the final detailing of wrinkles, creases, and folds. Give particular attention to final shaping of the head, jaw, ears, neck, and tusks. Each should be finish shaped and smoothed.

Features for final detailing on the elephant's head will include the patterning of the creases and wrinkles on the trunk, the final shape and smoothing of the tusks, ear folds, nostrils, and any other areas of the head that require finishing touches.

2. The creases are first cut in with a small inverted cone stone, starting on the top centerline of the trunk and cutting the wrinkle in one side and then the other. With a flame shaped stone, the edges of the wrinkles on the upper portion of the trunk are slightly rounded out to give the upper side of the crease a larger "rolled" look, while the lower portion of each crease shallows out away from the depth of the crease.

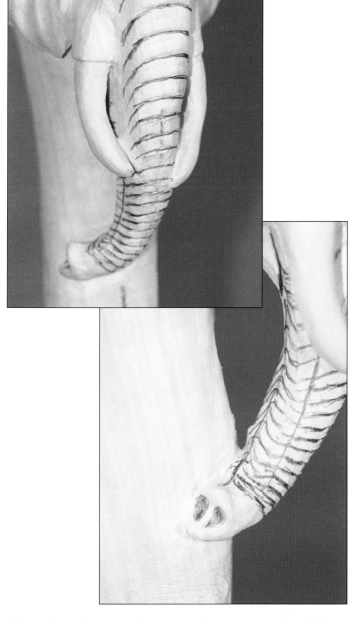

3. Draw the shape of the tip of the trunk before considering where the nostrils will be drawn. The finished shape of the tip of the trunk will determine the size of the nostrils. Shape the end of the trunk with a small flame shaped ruby carver. Slightly hollow the tip of the trunk to leave a rounded indentation where the nostrils will go (Honor the shape of the prehensile "finger" on the top of the tip of the trunk) — then draw the inverted teardrop shape of the nostrils.

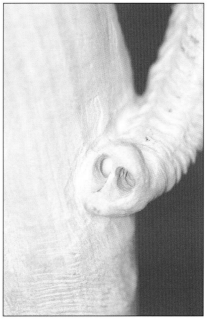

4. With a small diamond ball shaped bit, cut the shape of the nostrils within the hollow tip of the trunk. Once the roundness and depth of each nostril has been satisfied and each nostril is uniformly shaped one to the other, cut a shallow furrow from the bottom of each nostril hole out to the tip of the trunk using a drag stroke with a small flame shaped ruby carver.

1. Draw the trunk creases in the pattern and crease amounts desired (these vary from elephant to elephant, so you have a degree of latitude here).

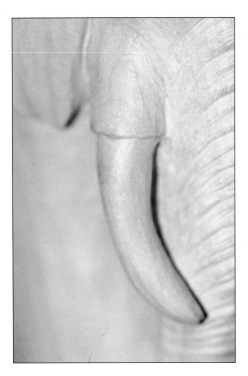

5. Round and smooth out the tusks to the length and shape that you want them – I used a tapered mandrel loaded with 400 grit sanding cloth. Honor the "ledge" of skin from the head that comes out over each tusk – keep them well defined and uniform.

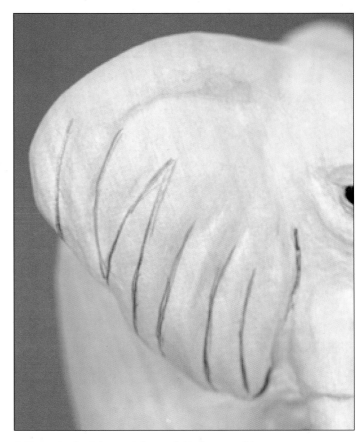

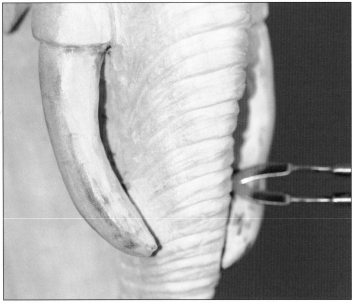

• To obtain a harder, smoother look to the tusks, I set a woodburning pen with a spear tip to run at a very low heat and "cauterized" the tusk surfaces by rubbing the tusks with the flat side of the pen.

6. Draw the final shape of the ear folds (some will be single line shaped, "V" shaped, or even "Y" shaped).

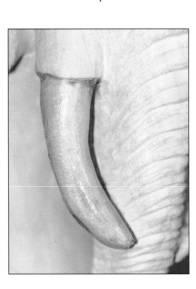

• To add strength to the tusks, cover them completely with a coat of super glue. This will impregnate the tusks and help strengthen them—or any deficiencies within or along the grain of the tusk.

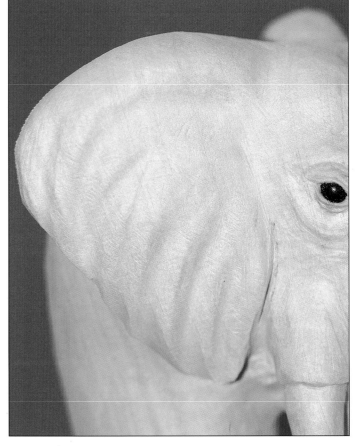

Finish shape the folds into a wavy pattern with the body of a flame shaped ruby carver, then finish shape all ear edges with a tapered mandrel loaded with 400 grit sanding cloth.

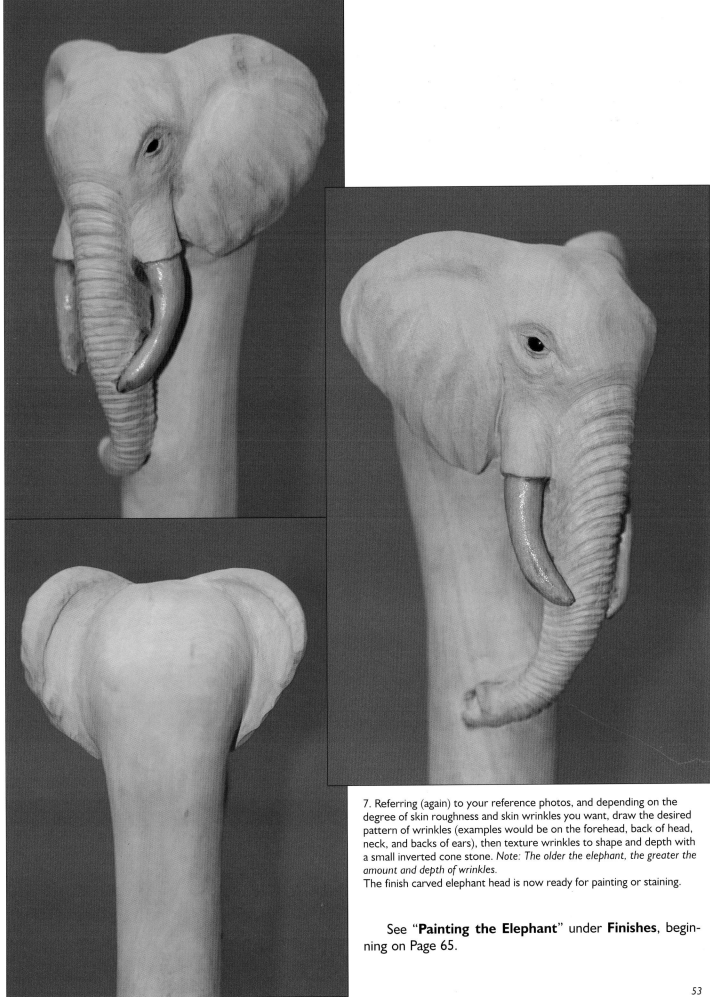

7. Referring (again) to your reference photos, and depending on the degree of skin roughness and skin wrinkles you want, draw the desired pattern of wrinkles (examples would be on the forehead, back of head, neck, and backs of ears), then texture wrinkles to shape and depth with a small inverted cone stone. *Note: The older the elephant, the greater the amount and depth of wrinkles.*

The finish carved elephant head is now ready for painting or staining.

See **"Painting the Elephant"** under **Finishes**, beginning on Page 65.

Carving a Rabbit Cane Head

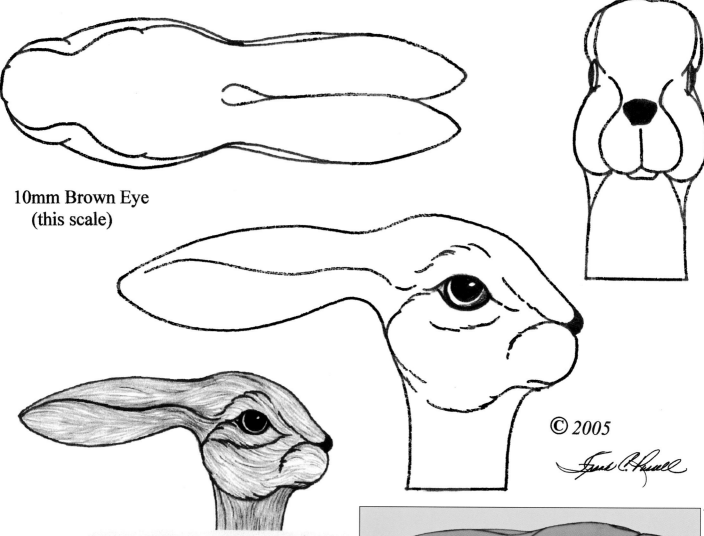

10mm Brown Eye
(this scale)

© 2005

Fur Flow Pattern

Preparing the Carving Block

Whenever possible, transfer the pattern to the carving block to reflect both the side view and the top view. Any shape, size, and detail presented by the outlines of both views will lend accuracy to the sawn out blank and greatly benefit in the carving sequences. Make sure that both pattern views are registered properly from top to bottom and from side to side.

*Always begin a cane head project such as this with an **accurately squared** block of stock. Cut the block to a size that will fit the pattern you have selected with just a bit to spare. A squared block is necessary to accurately drill a hole for the shaft, or a hole to receive hardware.*

1. Create a template by gluing the front and side pattern views to a piece of poster board or sheet plastic and carefully cutting them out. I prefer this method because I can use the pattern template over and over again. Some carvers just make an extra copy of the pattern, cut out the outline, glue the views to the block using a glue stick, then cut around the glued outline. This works if you don't plan to carve the same piece again. I prefer to keep the template patterns to use again or to share with students and carving friends.

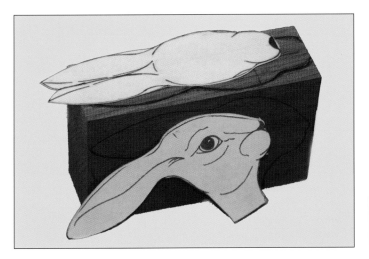

2. Transfer outline of the side and top views of the pattern to the carving block by drawing around the patterns.

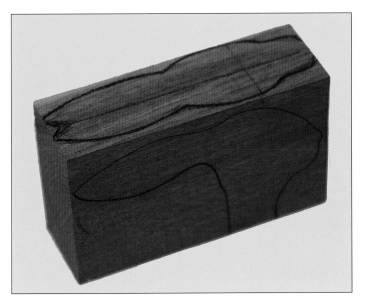

3. Make sure the top view and the side view are registered accurately one to the other. This is necessary for two reasons – first, to accurately saw the carving blank, and, second, to accurately locate and drill the receiving hole for the shaft or cane hardware.

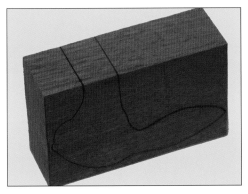

4. From the side view, extend the thickness of the neck across the bottom of the carving block. Carefully measure and mark the intersecting centers of the neck thickness and width of the block.

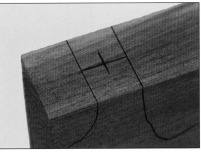

5. Select your choice of cane hardware.

6. Choose the size of drill bit to drill the receiving hole that will receive the cane shaft or cane hardware. If the cane shaft is to be permanently mounted (glued) in the cane handle, a Forstner bit of appropriate size to receive the cane shaft should be drilled in the handle. If cane hardware is to be used between the handle and the shaft, a drill bit of appropriate size to receive the hardware should be used.

7. Carefully register the drill on the center point of the receiving hole, and drill the hole.

1. Cut the side view outline (the side view is usually best to start with) with one continuous cut, leaving as much of the carving block as possible, intact. Preserving as much of the block outside the outline as possible not only preserves the outline of the top view for cutting, but also leaves support under and within the blank as the top view is being cut.

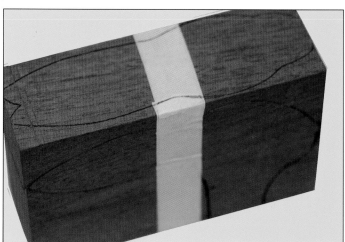

8. Fit the cane hardware to the hole. *Note: It is usually best **not** to glue the cane hardware in place until you are satisfied with the progress of the nearly completed carving.*

2. Put the sawn pieces back together and wrap a piece of masking tape around the entire assembly. Experience may allow you to hold the pieces firmly with your fingers as you saw, but safety dictates a wrap of masking tape. *You can usually see the drawn outline through the masking tape, but if not, re-mark the outline over the masking tape by drawing around the top view template.*

3. Saw the top view, leaving a portion of the masking tape to hold the pieces together where the tape has been wrapped across the front view.

1. Draw a centerline all around the carving, beginning at a point on the front, then up over the head, down the center of the back of the neck and back to the point of beginning. Whenever the carving process removes the centerline, replace it, as it is extremely important to maintaining symmetry while carving.

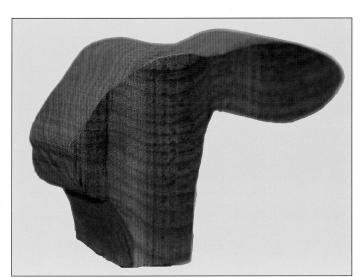

4. Holding the blank with fingers away from the saw blade, finish cutting through the masking tape on both sides of the front view. Discard waste pieces.

Rough Carving the Blank

When roughing out, always be aware of the amount of stock that you are removing. Leaving more stock than necessary is the safest route. You can always remove stock as you go – it is tough to replace if you remove too much.

As the head is being rounded out, make every effort to achieve a symmetrical roundness and shape without any flat areas and without any squarish corners. The major mark of a beginner is a squarish looking carving, primarily due to the fear of removing too much stock. Study the subject through reference photos, videos, or if possible, in the flesh, to ascertain the natural shape (and grace) of your subject.

2. Draw all detail control lines for the contours and major details of the head. Give particular attention to the nose, mouth, forehead, eye mounds, ears, and shape of the jaw – these are all highpoints to this carving. Draw the general shape of the hollows and folds of the ears and the area where they join the head.

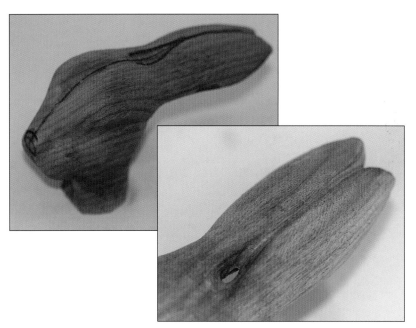

5. Glue one half of the joiner plate into the receiving hole of the neck with epoxy glue. Use care not to allow excess glue to spread onto the plate or threads.

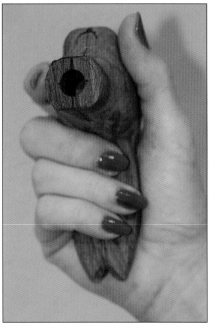

3. With a large flame shaped carbide bit, rough shape the major contours of the carving. Round out the jowls, cheeks, and neck with a medium flame shaped carbide bit. At this point, consideration should be given to the shape of the ears, not only from the standpoint of aesthetics (looks), but of functionality (use). The tops of the ears should be rounded to look like ears lying side by side, but also should be rounded so as to fit comfortably into the palm of the user. The underside of the ears should be carved in such a way that the hollows of the ears, not only look realistic, but also allow the user's fingers to fall comfortably into the hollow of the ear on the thumb side of the cane head.

6. After the epoxy glue sets, carefully wrap a piece of plastic electrician's tape around the plate of the joiner where it meets the bottom of the neck. *The tape is to protect the edge of the joiner plate from being nicked or marred by the bit as the excess stock surrounding the joiner plate is carved away.*

7. With a large tapered steel bit, remove the excess stock from around the joiner plate. Remove small amounts of stock, achieving as accurate and smooth a mating surface to the round joiner plate as possible.

8. Texture the area around the base of the neck where the neck and the joiner plate meet. *Note where the inverted cone texturing bit has nicked the tape, but left no mark on the edge of the brass plate.* Texture to a safe distance away from the disc and bottom of the neck, remove tape, and clean with a rotary brush.

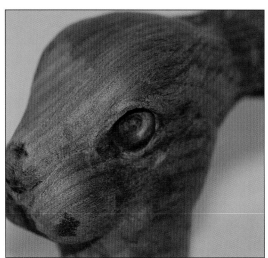

4. Locate eyes and carve eye cavities with a ball shaped ruby carver.

Finish Carving and Detailing

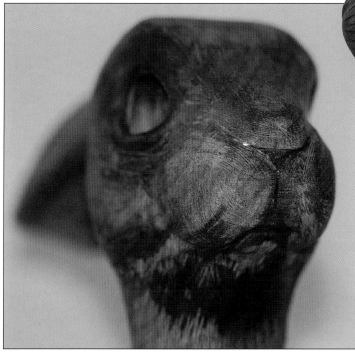

1. Draw nostrils, septum, and separation of upper and lower jaws (mouth line) to finished shape.

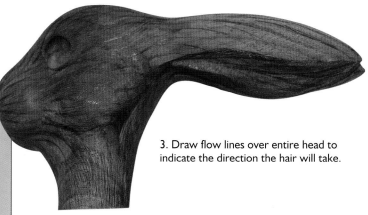

3. Draw flow lines over entire head to indicate the direction the hair will take.

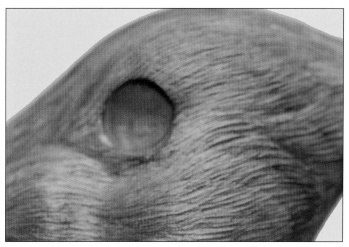

4. Texture the head using a medium to large inverted cone shaped stone bit for most of the head, and a small inverted cone shaped stone for the muzzle and inner ears. *Be sure to texture at least the area around the eyes **before** bedding the eyes – one miss-stroke touching an eye with a texturing stone will mar the eye and ruin the looks of the carving.*

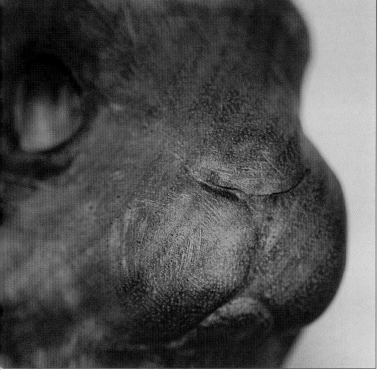

2. With a small flame shaped diamond bit, carve nostril shapes and indentations. *To achieve the "comma" shape of each nostril, lay a small flame shaped diamond bit in the bottom of each nostril hole and cut in the "tail" of the nostril on each side to form the opposing comma shapes of the nostrils.* Holding the small flame shaped diamond bit at a low angle and using a drag stroke, cut in the line of the mouth. Finish shaping the nose, septum, lips, and mouth corners with smoothing strokes using a tapered stone bit.

5. To bed the eyes and model the eyelids, I use Quikwood® epoxy wood repair putty. This material gives sufficient time to model eyes within about thirty minutes. If you anticipate using more time than this, mix enough to do only one eye at a time. I prefer Quikwood® to bed eyes on carvings, especially where I want to match a natural finish, because it readily accepts wood stains that will match the wood color I have used.

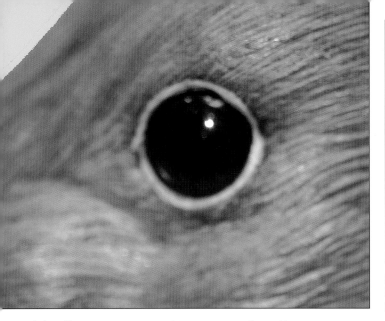

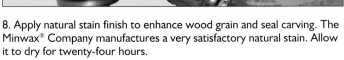

8. Apply natural stain finish to enhance wood grain and seal carving. The Minwax® Company manufactures a very satisfactory natural stain. Allow it to dry for twenty-four hours.

6. Install eyes, using care to achieve symmetry from side to side, top to bottom, and from front to rear. I used glass taxidermy eyes on this project because they, over other glass eyes, helped achieve the look I wanted for the cane head.
Note A: *Set glass eyes as described in the "Setting Glass Eyes" section on page 31.*
Note B: *Clean entire carving with a rotary brush to remove any and all debris left by the carving and/or wood burning process. Use care as any particles of dust will be sealed to the carving and are sure to show up during any staining or painting process.*

9. Complete the carving with two or more coats of a good exterior polyurethane finish.

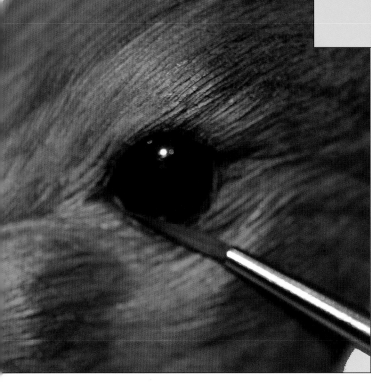

7. Stain eyelids with a stain to match the wood used for the carving – because I used black walnut to carve the head, in this case I used *Special Walnut* by the Minwax® Company.

    The 3/4" diameter shaft for the rabbit cane head was constructed of a matching black walnut dowel. The finish was applied in the same manner as the rabbit head, enhancing the grain with a natural stain, then finishing with several coats of gloss polyurethane finish.
    Once the shaft was cut to length to fit its new owner, the shaft tip was equipped with a trekking stick tip that allows the use of either a rubber tip for house and dry street use, or a pointed steel tip for use on rough, slippery terrain.

Finishing

Cleaning

As previously stated, upon completion of the hair or fur texturing process, whether stone grinding texture or wood burning texture, it is imperative that the carving be cleaned completely. I find the large soft-bristled rotary brush with a diameter of from two-inches to four-inches ideal for cleaning any carving that I have done.

For those without a rotary brush to clean debris from a carving, a soft toothbrush scrubbed and swept in the direction of the texture lines will suffice, but will take somewhat longer.

Keep in mind that it is of absolute importance that the carving be as clean as possible before it is sealed! If any of the tiny bits of grinding dust from stone texturing or char dust from wood burner texturing are left on the surface of the carving and not removed, they will be locked in place forever when the sealer is applied. These lumps may not be readily visible upon the initial application of the sealer, but when gesso is applied, they will pull more gesso from the brush than the surrounding surface and each lump will become magnified. When the paint is applied, especially if applied with a manual brush, they tend to enlarge even more, and will be quite noticeable when under a strong light or natural sunlight.

The best, and most unforgiving, light used to check for existing dirt prior to sealing is morning sunlight. Not only will this type of light reveal dirt, but also very often I find other things to correct on the carving. That is why I call it an unforgiving light – if imperfections exist, this light is relentless in its ability to reveal imperfections in a carving when the carving is turned and viewed at different angles.

Sealing

I seal all of my carvings with acrylic automotive lacquer. Thin the lacquer with lacquer thinner at a ratio of *50% lacquer* to *50% lacquer thinner*. I apply the thinner with a large natural bristle brush, and allow the carving to accept as much as possible without losing any texture detail. The deeper the sealer penetrates, the better. I never use a commercially prepared sanding sealer, due to problems I have had in the past with it filling and obliterating texture detail. The next choice is Deft™ satin polyurethane cut in the same 50/50 proportions with lacquer thinner.

Paint

For *manual brush application*, it makes little difference what acrylic paint manufacturer you use, as long as that particular paint, its consistency, and range of colors satisfies you and is compatible with the manner in which you apply color. If you are like most, it will take a while for you to "settle in" to the manufacturer of a paint that satisfies you the most. There is one that I consider too "slippery" as it comes off the brush and is blended – yet many of my fellow carvers swear by it. Another just feels too gritty and dry as it is blended and I just don't feel comfortable with it – yet it is preferred over all by other woodcarvers. There are even some reds and oranges by one manufacturer that I like better than another, yet I dislike their earth colors. Experience and use will establish a preference. I finally settled on the Grumbacher™ and Liquitex™ brands for what my needs require for manual brush application.

For *airbrush color application* on woodcarvings, I use Holbein Aeroflash™, Golden™, or Badger™ liquid acrylic color – or a combination thereof. I used and experimented with several different brands of acrylic paints manufactured specifically for airbrushes and enjoyed only limited success. I was looking for smoothness and consistency in a pre-mixed liquid that I, as well as my students, could use over extended periods of time without clogging an airbrush or causing undue drying or crusting on the tips of the airbrushes.

Experiment with different paints until you find one that suits your method and style of application. A few considerations relevant to suitable use would be ease of application, smoothness, durability, and the most forgiving mixture of airbrush paint from a manufacturer who offers the widest choice of both opaque and transparent colors. On a long-term basis, considerations such as these presented the fewest problems whether I was using an airbrush alone or with a group in an instructional setting where trouble free application is imperative.

Stain

Unless I actually have to, I use *only* a grain enhancer such as Minwax© Natural Stain (see *Carving the Rabbit Head Cane*) to bring out the beauty of the grain in the carving to which I am applying finish.

If I have to use stain on bland woods such as Basswood, Tupelo, or Poplar, I add thin coats of stain until I get the depth of color that I want. I allow each coat to dry thoroughly before I add the next coat, which I feel gives me maximum penetration. If I am staining for a walnut finish, I stain until I get a surface that looks like walnut, instead of a basswood surface that looks like it has a coat of walnut stain over it

Finish

There are many excellent finishes on the market with which to give a final and appealing protective coating to a cane or walking stick. Of the choices available, I have used deck enamel, marine varnishes, polyurethanes in flat, matte, and gloss finishes. The new marine clear finishes have provided the best longevity when subjected to the roughest abuse over any given terrain. Most of the canes I have carved are finished with several thinned coats of matte finish polyurethane, which provides satisfactory finish for canes subjected to normal use

Painting Materials and Techniques

Manual Brush

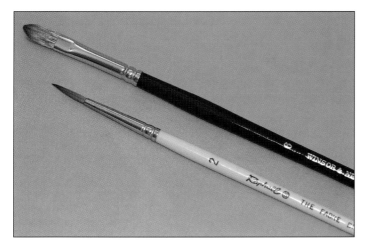

Only two types of brushes were used for the projects throughout this book. One was a round Kolinsky sable brush and the other was a sable bristled Filbert brush. Although the sizes of the brushes varied from project to project, the type of brush and quality remained the same.

There is an axiom about brushes that I have found to be true for the whole of my carving and painting career, and that is: **Buy the best brush that you can afford**. Nothing performs better than a quality brush, and if properly used, nothing seems to last longer than a quality brush.

I have found the Raphael© and Windsor-Newton© brushes to be the most to my liking, with the higher quality lines of Holbein© and Grumbacher© brushes also giving excellent results. I'm sure there are other brush companies who make brushes as suitable as those mentioned, but the manufacturers named above make brushes I have used, have confidence in, have proven quality, and have all found a place in my brush box.

A good brush should be cared for and treated with the attention that any fine tool should receive to insure long-life.

Before I subject any of my brushes to the paint on my palette, I dunk them in the medium that I will be using to thin my paint. If it is oil paint, I first dunk the brush in turpentine; if it is acrylic paint, I first dunk the brush in water. I was once told by an art teacher to allow the ferrule to fill with the thinning medium first, which will keep pure paint from going into the ferrule and clogging the ferrule, which will eventually displace the bristles to the point that the brush will be deformed.

Brushes should be thoroughly cleaned and dried after use. I use a gentle sudsy mixture of washing liquid and warm wa-

ter, then I rinse thoroughly with clean warm water. After partially drying, I reshape each brush with my lips, and store vertically with the bristles up in a container, or roll several brushes in a thick piece of cloth the size of a place mat and store horizontally.

As I use a brush, especially a round brush, I hold the manufacturer's name upward in my grip while I paint. This may seem odd, but I believe through use, the bristles become conditioned to being used in the same manner each time, and therefore *perform* in the same manner each time

Airbrush

As with a manual brush, choose the best airbrush you can afford that not only performs in all areas of comfort and use in the manner you prefer, but also an airbrush that gives the result you want with the least amount of effort. Current MSRPs (manufacturer suggested retail prices) run anywhere from $25 to well over $500, so along with an extremely wide range of price, the beginning airbrush user has just as wide a range of quality, function, and performance to consider.

In the twenty years that I have used airbrushes, and for the ten years that I have taught airbrush techniques to my students, I have come to depend on several different airbrush manufacturers. I have given students a choice of these airbrushes to use as part of their painting classes – and also made them available for purchase by the students at the end of each class. To do this, I had to gain confidence in every airbrush model through personal use before I would equip a painting station – let alone recommend or allow the unit to be used by a student in a classroom situation.

I soon came to favor the Iwata HP series airbrushes. I was given an earlier model of the Iwata HPC airbrush by a friend about fifteen years ago, and it has remained my "gun" of choice to this day. I have yet to replace a part, and I have painted everything from miniature carvings to carousel horses with it. It has been used with virtually every kind of medium for about every kind of work from stenciling bathroom walls to painting my old four-wheel drive truck with my favorite camouflaging pattern.

The Iwata HP (High Performance) Series has long been an indispensable workhorse for amateur and professionals alike and is available in three color cup sizes. The choice of one or the other will depend pretty much on the degree of viscosity and quantity of medium you want available to "throw" without reloading.

Now called the HP-Plus, the pleasure this airbrush provides while in use is now more noticeably supported by, and because of, features and specifications that include:

- Dual-purpose, cutaway and pre-set handle for easy clean up and precise control of paint flow.
- Teflon™ needle packing for automotive and/or other solvent-based paints.
- Larger threads on the nozzle offer a more secure fit and better centering of the nozzle.
- Redesigned tapered gravity-feed cups also ensure easy clean-up and a more efficient paint flow.
- Single-piece auxiliary lever/needle-chucking guide provide easy assembly.
- Each nozzle is precisely made on the industry's most sophisticated machinery, then hand tested to assure accurate control and fine atomization of the spray.
- Each nozzle is self-sealing, which eliminates the need for messy sealer.
- The steel-alloy nozzles are more durable and resist damage from harsh chemicals better than do conventional brass nozzles.

HP-A Plus

Features a 0.2-mm nozzle and needle combination for high-precision, detail spraying. The 1/32-oz. color cup is integrated in the barrel forward of the trigger, and works very well where lesser amounts of a thinner medium are used. Excellent for everything from detailing fur and feathers on larger carvings to the gun of choice to completely finish miniature woodcarvings and dioramas.

HP-B Plus

Features a 0.2 nozzle and needle combination and supports the same features as the HP-A Plus but with a larger 1/16-oz. gravity feed color cup for greater medium capacity.

HP-C Plus

A practical choice for most airbrush uses, the larger 1/3-oz. gravity feed color cup and larger 0.3-mm needle/nozzle combination allows the HP-C Plus to be used with most media. Capable of from fine hairline to finely atomized background spray, it also features an entire range of stippling effects. The larger color cup is useful for "on gun" mixing of custom colors, and allows for quick color changes. The short paint passageway from the color cup to the nozzle gives it a responsive feel and allows it to be one of the quickest cleaning airbrushes available.

I have used an HPC model airbrush over fifteen years for personal use and have also had one at each painting station at my school for the last several years.

For a catalog or additional information about any Iwata-Medea airbrush, accessory, or product contact:

Iwata-Medea Company
79 SE Taylor Street
Portland, OR 97214
www.iwata-medea.com

Airbrush Cleaning

The main performance problem I have had with any airbrush is when a student is lax about cleaning, and with airbrushes as forgiving as the ones described that usually doesn't take too long to remedy.

Again, the greatest problem encountered with *any* airbrush is that of not keeping the airbrush properly cleaned. Hopefully, the airbrush you are using is of the highest quality available to you and should therefore continue to serve as long as it is kept clean.

At first, cleaning between color changes may seem to be a chore, but soon it will become so much a part of the painting routine that it is done automatically and with little thought.

If you ever have cause to use an airbrush that has been improperly cared for, you will soon realize and appreciate why cleaning an airbrush is a second-nature function. Refer to the owner's manual acompanying the airbrush of your choice for specific directions with regard to its cleaning and care.

Applying Color

To maintain control over color, whether it is being applied with a manual brush or an airbrush, it should be applied in thin layers.

When applying color with a manual brush, it should *never* be applied directly from the tube, but should be mixed with an appropriate thinning medium (i.e.: water for acrylics, turpentine for oils) so as to provide an even, controllable coat of color. It may take several washes (for acrylics) of color to attain the depth and tone of color desired. For example, by applying washes of color, the depth of color can be brought up to a certain level by using darker shades or it can be brought down by using lighter shades of the same color.

With exception of some of the gesso coating applied with a filbert brush, and some miniscule highlight/touch-up lines, the elephant below was painted entirely with an airbrush.

Painting the African Elephant

Color Mixing

Before applying any color to the carving, mix paint to the color of gray that you would choose if you only had **one** color of gray to paint the elephant – this will be called the *base color*. I arrived at the shade of gray that I wanted for this elephant cane head by mixing different combinations of Titanium White, Black, and Burnt Umber, then holding them against photographs and mixing until I matched what I considered a representative color – as a proportion for this mixture I ended up with 90% Titanium White, 5% Black, and 5% Burnt Umber.

You may have manufacturer's colors that are stronger or weaker, but start with the above proportion and mix lighter or darker to satisfy the shade that *you* prefer.

You have quite a bit of latitude when it comes to this selection of gray – elephants seem to run from a brownish gray to a medium-light gray.

I use this method of color mixing for any carving that I am about to paint that I do not already have a proven color schematic for. Once I find the combination I like, I make notes on proportions, and file them away for future use. These notes

1. Seal carving completely with clear matte finish acrylic automotive lacquer or Deft© matte finish. Thin the lacquer or Deft 50/50 with lacquer thinner. Allow carving to absorb all the thinned lacquer it will take.

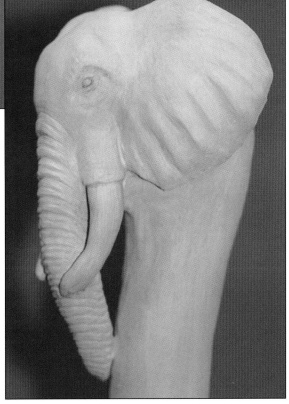

2. Gesso entire carving with several coats of thinned gesso. I prefer to apply gesso with a stiff bristle brush using a scrubbing motion that forces the gesso particles into the detail of the carving. The gesso should be of a coffee-cream consistency, which will allow the color of the wood to show through on the first coat. Apply thin coats until the entire surface of the carving is an opaque white. Note: I paint over glass eyes during the entire seal, gesso, and color application process for two reasons. First, it saves time; secondly, it gives me greater freedom and continuity for painting lines and/or shadows through or around the eyes – without having to stop from one corner of the eye to the other.

have saved me time and effort for countless carvings of birds and animals to say nothing of human skin tones, eye shades, and hair shades.

I mixed this base color in twice the amount I would normally use on the carving for two reasons.

- First, so I could take a quarter of the amount and mix it up to a highlight color by adding more white (with a touch of raw umber) and using it to highlight elevated areas on the carving that would appear lighter.

- Secondly, so I could take another quarter of the amount and to mix it down to the shadow/shading color by adding more black/burnt umber as the shade color to be used in all deepened areas of the carving that would normally appear darker. Color should be heavier in the crevices and thin out to nothing as it approaches the highlighted high points but you first need the base color to blend through.

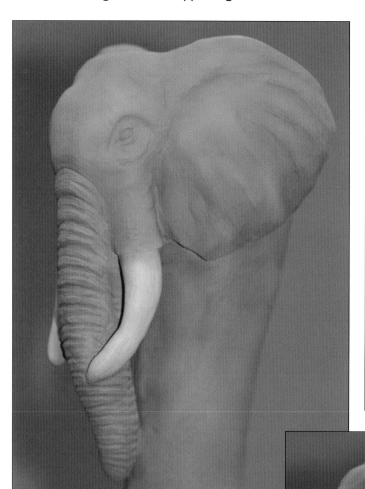

1. Begin by covering the entire head (excluding the tusks) with the base color. I often experiment with the color at this stage with heavier to light application just to get a feel for shading and highlighting. Apply color in thin layers until the desired depth of color is achieved.

2. With the shading color, shadow all areas where the base color would appear darker on the real animal. Blend the shadow color into the base color. (Some shaded or darkened areas for consideration would be behind and under the ear folds, under the trunk, around the eyes, and depressed contours on the head) *One way to ascertain where shading/ shadows and highlights should fall is to observe the carving by rotating it horizontally in a medium to strong light source – when I can, I use natural sunlight.*

3. With the highlighting color, carefully apply a lighter hue to areas of the carving that you determine should look lighter. Again, use light blending to allow the edges of the highlight to thin and disappear into the base or shadow coloring. (Some highlighted areas for consideration would be the top of any mounded area on the head, the top of the trunk, high points of the ears, and any other raised contour that would catch light)

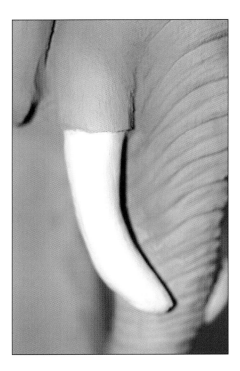

4. Mix a combination of white, (with a tiny touch of raw umber to soften the glare of the white) to get the tusk base color. Cover the tusks entirely with this mixture. They may appear extremely white at this point, but the next step will tone them down.

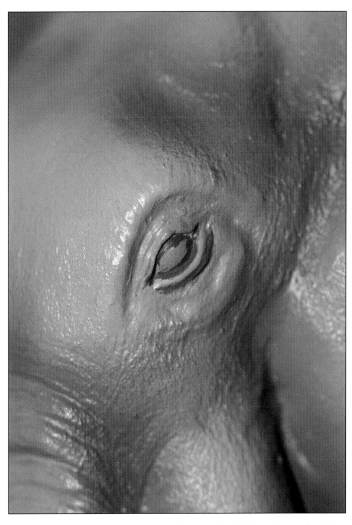

5. Thin out burnt umber (transparent) with flow medium or water until it is almost the consistency of ink. Very sparingly apply some around the base of the tusk where it protrudes from the head. (Little air and little color if you are using an airbrush, and a blending almost dry brush if you are using a manual brush). A shadowing effect can also be achieved by using the same color very lightly applied to the bottom curvature of the tusks.

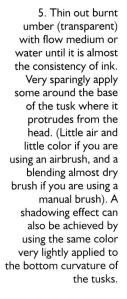

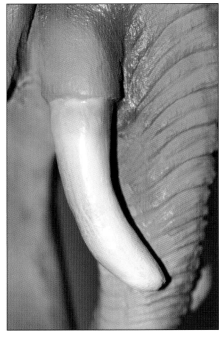

7. Using the same dark gray color and a round sable brush or airbrush, accentuate any deep wrinkles or creases that require fine line accentuation – ex: around the eyes, ear folds near the body, and miniscule lines on the trunk.

8. Coat the entire carving with a protective covering of one or more coats of matte or flat finish lacquer or polyurethane. I put a heavy coat on all my cane heads to protect the painted surface from hand wear. Sometimes I get more shine than I want, even with a flat or "satin" finish – but, I'd rather have shine with the protective coating than no shine and have the paint wear off. If I get too much of a plastic look, as a final coat, I will spray the entire finished carving with Testor's® flat coat spray that I get from the local hobby shop.

6. Paint the inside of the nostrils with a dark gray color.

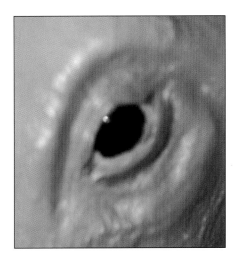

9. Remove paint from the eyes by outlining with an Xacto® or pointed scalpel-type blade. Cut around the inside of the eyelid with the point, then, cut around the eye with the flat of the blade. Finish cleaning the residue with the dowel modeling tool that was used to set the eye. If necessary, replace the black inner ring of the eye and re-clean the eye.

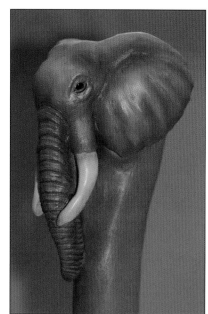

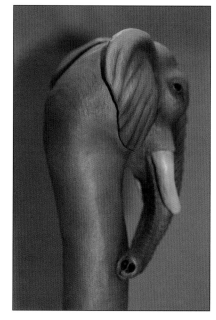

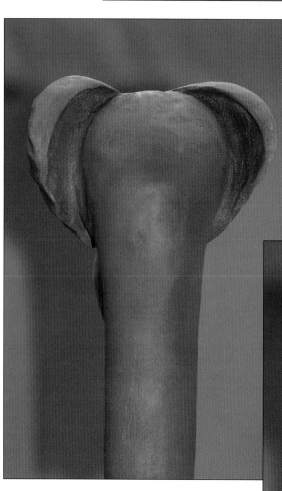

10. Finished elephant head.

Project Patterns and Plans

Horn X-section

7mm Brown Eye
(this scale)

BIGHORN SHEEP

© 2002

7mm Brown Eye
(this scale)

BISON © 2002 *Frank C. Russell*

7mm Brown Eye
(this scale)

CHIMPANZEE © 2002 *Frank C. Russell*

DRAFT HORSE

© 2001

7mm Brown Eye
(this scale)

7mm Brown Eye
(this scale)

GOLDEN RETRIEVER

© 2001

8mm Brown Eye
(this scale)

GRIZZLY BEAR

© 2002

GROUND HOG/MARMOT

Tail Detail

4mm Brown Eye
(this scale)

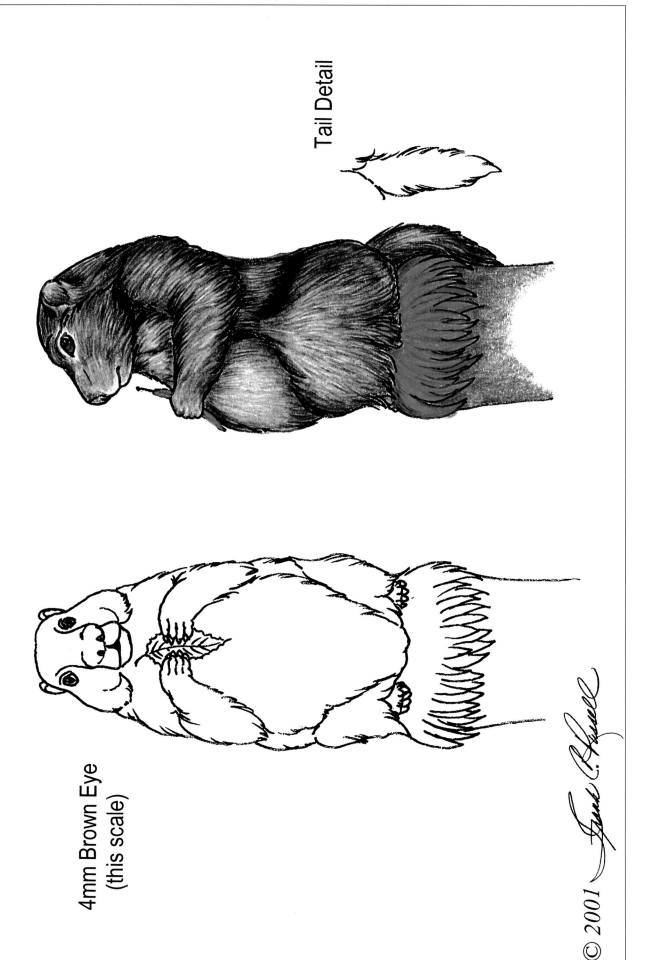

© 2001

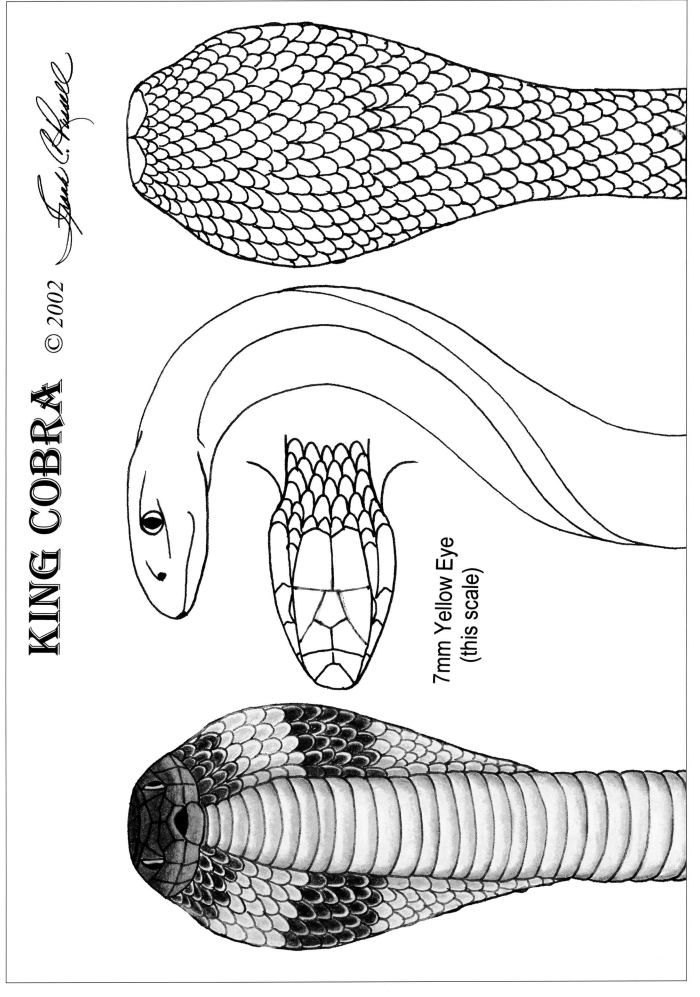

KING COBRA © 2002

7mm Yellow Eye
(this scale)

Calm

8mm Yellow Eye
(this scale)

LION

Snarling

© 2002

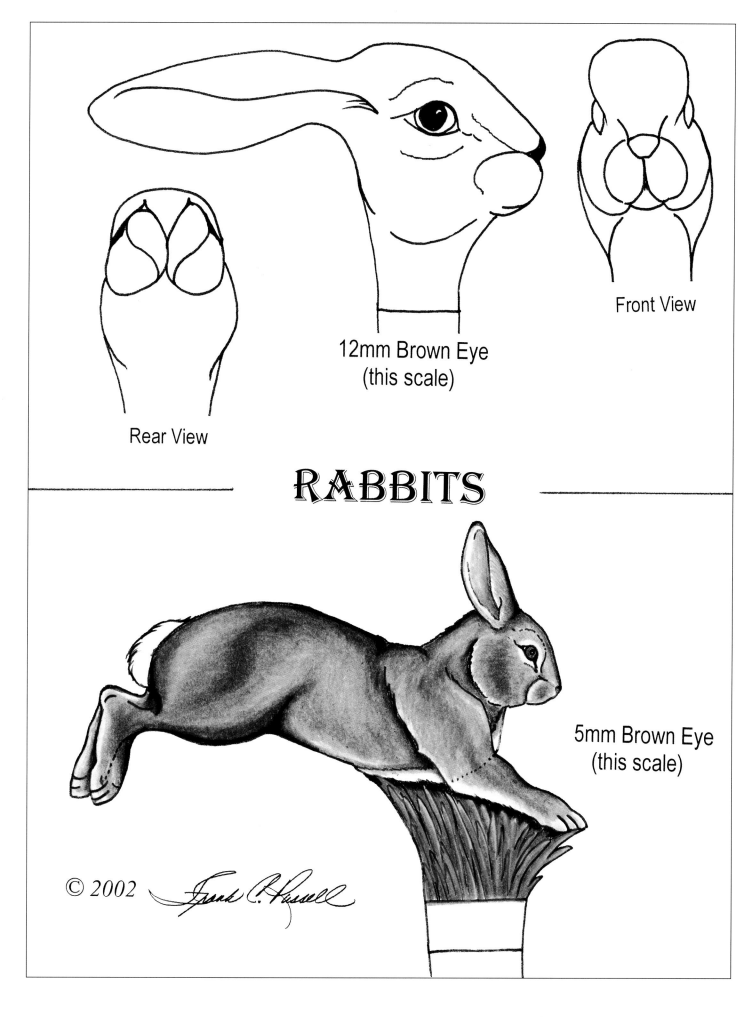

Rear View

12mm Brown Eye
(this scale)

Front View

RABBITS

5mm Brown Eye
(this scale)

© 2002 Frank C. Russell

5mm Brown Eye
(this scale)

RED SQUIRREL

© 2001

Calm

8mm Yellow Eye
(this scale)

TIGER

Snarling

WALRUS

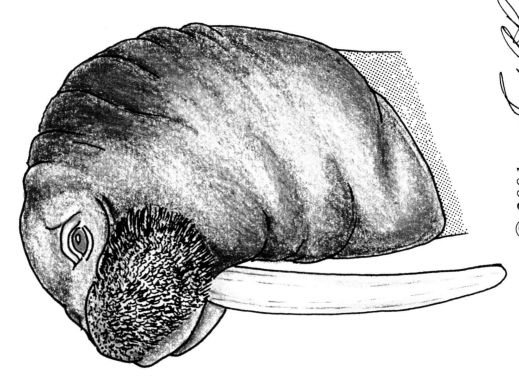

© 2001

10MM Brown Eyes
(this scale)

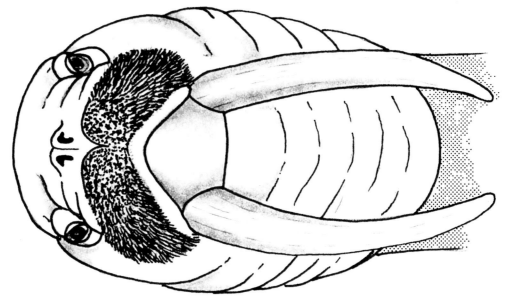